STOMPING OUT DEPRESSION

Neil T. Anderson
and Dave Park

Regal

From Gospel Light
Ventura, California, U.S.A.

Published by Regal Books
Gospel Light
Ventura, California, U.S.A.
Printed in the U.S.A.

Regal Books is a ministry of Gospel Light, an evangelical Christian publisher dedicated to serving the local church. We believe God's vision for Gospel Light is to provide church leaders with biblical, user-friendly materials that will help them evangelize, disciple and minister to children, youth and families.

It is our prayer that this Regal book will help you discover biblical truth for your own life and help you meet the needs of others. May God richly bless you.

For a free catalog of resources from Regal Books/Gospel Light, please call your Christian supplier or contact us at 1-800-4-GOSPEL or www.regalbooks.com.

Cover and Inside Design by Robert Williams
Edited by Steven Lawson

LIBRARY OF CONGRESS CATALOGING-IN-PUBLICATION DATA
Anderson, Neil T., 1942-
  Stomping out depression/ Neil T. Anderson and Dave Park.
    p. cm.
  Includes bibliographical references.
  ISBN 0-8307-2892-9
  1. Christian teenagers—Religious life. 2. Depression in adolescence—Religious aspects—Christianity. I. Park, Dave, 1961 - II. Title.
  BV4531.3 .A54 2001
  248.8'6—dc21   2001048543

  2 3 4 5 6 7 8 9 10 11 12 13 14 15 / 09 08 07 06 05 04

Rights for publishing this book in other languages are contracted by Gospel Light Worldwide, the international nonprofit ministry of Gospel Light. Gospel Light Worldwide also provides publishing and technical assistance to international publishers dedicated to producing Sunday School and Vacation Bible School curricula and books in the languages of the world. For additional information, visit www.gospellightworldwide.org; write to Gospel Light Worldwide, P.O. Box 3875, Ventura, CA 93006; or send an e-mail to info@gospellightworldwide.org.

CONTENTS

FOREWORD

by Josh McDowell

Young people today often define their life experiences in terms of being "extreme" or "real." To see this, all we have to do is look at the popularity of extreme sports and reality television. As I have spoken to hundreds of thousands of young people through the years, I have found that while the words have changed, this sentiment has not: The seemingly limitless energy of youth that lifts you to the greatest highs can also take you to the deepest lows.

Much is written about the good times, the achievements and the creative thrust of young people. But very little has been done to address the hard times. Understandably, young people prefer to focus on the best moments of life. Few want to talk about what happens when your world collapses, or at least you think it has. No one wants to deal head on with one of the greatest problems young people face: depression. Yet, for all too many, it is very real.

Several years back, Neil T. Anderson and Dave Park developed two much-needed books—*Stomping Out the Darkness* and *The Bondage Breaker*, Youth Edition. These excellent resources point you to the one place where you can gain your true identity and freedom. Your commitment to the Word of God and careful study will help you realize the power of your identity in Christ and help you become the spiritual person you want to be. These two books are great places to begin.

How wonderful that Neil and Dave have now extended their work to specifically shed insights into how youth can win their battles with depression. In this new book, *Stomping Out Depression*, Neil and Dave demystify what has for too long been relegated to the shadows of youth culture. Standing against the real spiritual forces of this fallen world and learning how to win the struggle for the mind is a message for today's youth and people of all ages.

Loss, hopelessness and helplessness are words a depressed youth knows very well. Here Neil and Dave show how, when you know who you are in Christ, you can fully confront and overcome the agony and find freedom from depression.

Stomping Out Depression provides real answers for an extreme condition. It is must reading for every person who has ever waded into the debilitating waters of depression, and it provides "must answers" for every person who wants out of its harrowing depths. The pages that follow provide a path to finding hope again.

ACKNOWLEDGMENTS

Writing a book is a difficult task, especially when your desire is to help hurting people. We as humans are fearfully and wonderfully made and not one of us is exactly like another. Our prayer is that the truths and principles contained in this book will help you find hope again. First and foremost, we thank our awesome God and heavenly Father for His love and calling in our lives. We have sensed His presence as we prepared each paragraph, and we acknowledge that without Him, we are nothing. Second, we thank our wives, Joanne and Grace. Their love, patience, support and encouragement have not only improved the quality of this book but also made us into better husbands and people.

We thank Hal Baumchen for his work on *Finding Hope Again*, the catalyst for this work. We are indebted to all those who shared their stories with us. We wish to especially acknowledge Alice Gray for the wonderful stories she gathered in her book *Stories for the Extreme Teen's Heart* and for granting us permission to reprint a few of them. Our hearts have been enriched because of these wonderful testimonies. We also want to thank Josh McDowell for his tremendous support and for writing the foreword.

We thank Bill Greig III and Kyle Duncan for their patience and support of this project. Special thanks go to Steven Lawson—you make us look good. Your professionalism has truly enriched this book. It has been a blessing to work with all the fine staff at Regal, including Kim Bangs, Deena Davis, Rose Decaen, Nola Grunden, George Keenen, Elizabeth Lubaczewski, Bayard Taylor, Hilary Young, Pam Weston and Rob Williams. Our thanks to you for making this book possible. May the Lord use it to His honor and glory!

Neil T. Anderson and Dave Park

INTRODUCTION

Picking up a book such as *Stomping Out Depression* might make you feel funny; you might even feel a sense of shame. Well, don't!

There is no shame in feeling depressed. It is an inevitable part of growing up. Everyone at some time in his or her life will face the challenge of depression. In too many cases pride prevents us from seeking the help we need, and the consequences are often predictable and tragic. As the Bible makes clear, pride comes before a fall, and God is opposed to pride.

The fact that you have picked up this book and are now reading through it signals the beginning of dependency on Christ and a deathblow to self-sufficiency and pride. Only people who are secure in Christ can readily admit their need for one another, and they do not hesitate to ask for help when they need it.

If you are struggling with depression, there is hope. We wrote this book to help you establish your hope in God. We want to enable you to live and walk according to His truth, rather than the circumstances that surround you. We want to extend to you the mercy and the wonderful grace of God. If hopelessness and despair have crept into your life and found a place in your belief system, we want to show you how to kick them out. It is our desire that you adopt a biblical view of reality, a true picture of what is happening in your life, and allow the truth of God to restore hope.

The process of renewal might seem difficult and even impossible right now, but it is not. That lie is just part of Satan's plan to keep you in bondage to hopelessness and depression. In this book you will read about others whose depression almost destroyed them, but their hope was awakened. They had their joy, peace and happiness in life restored to them. This turnaround in their lives can happen in yours! We will share many stories about people who found their freedom from depression. Their names have been changed, except for some who wanted to share openly their testimonies of finding freedom in Christ.

For the sake of smooth reading, we usually use "we" without distinguishing whether we are writing in Neil's or Dave's voice. When the text requires it to be one voice, we use "I" and then place the name of the person, either Neil or Dave, in parentheses.

It is the cry of our hearts that you would find hope again as Jesus stomps out your depression!

CHAPTER 1

FINDING HOPE

A cheerful disposition is good for your health; gloom and doom leave you bone-tired.

PROVERBS 17:22, *THE MESSAGE*

Laughter is the sun that drives winter from the human face.

VICTOR HUGO

Jan was an 18-year-old dynamo. She seemed to be able to do it all. She was a straight-A student, captain of the cheerleading squad, a volleyball player and homecoming queen. Everything seemed to be going great until Chad came along. Jan and Chad had been dating for about a year and a half. The relationship had started early in their junior year but now, after 18 months, it was over.

The day after the breakup, Jan met with some of her friends at Jock Rock in front of the school.

"I can't believe he broke up with me," Jan said. "And he did it over the phone—he didn't even have enough class to meet me in person and say it to my face."

"I say you're better off without the creep," Ashley said.

"Don't call him a creep," Jan stammered, fighting back the tears.

Morgan spoke up: "Hey, Jan, snap out of it. Everybody breaks up. It's not the end of the world. Besides, a girl like you could get a hundred boyfriends."

"Yeah," Ashley agreed. "If Chad doesn't want to have anything to do with you, then you should decide that you don't want to have anything to do with him. Besides, everybody breaks up—you just have to get over it and move on, girl."

"Hey, I heard that the new kid, Jason Watson, is available, and he's cute. Don't you think?" Morgan offered.

Jan didn't answer. She just turned and walked away without a word.

They don't understand, she thought to herself. *I don't want a new boyfriend—I want Chad.*

Chad was Jan's first real boyfriend, and she was planning to marry him after they graduated this year. Hundreds of times she had dreamed about the wedding. She would put flowers in her hair and walk down the hallway at home. She would turn to the teddy-bear preacher and say her vows.

Jan looked down sadly at the class ring on her finger and remembered the day Chad had first put it there. From that day she had decided that she would be everything that Chad wanted. She had dieted to stay skinny and dressed with him in mind. She had tried so hard to make him happy and do whatever she could to please him. When Chad began to pressure her to go all the way sexually, she decided to give him what he wanted. She wanted to make him happy.

When Chad broke up with her, Jan was devastated. She could not believe it; she had given him everything. She begged and pleaded with him not to leave her. She told him that she would do anything if he would just stay. But he refused to listen to her and hung up the phone. Jan had tried to call Chad several times but got no answer.

Jan's first reaction was anger. *Why won't he even talk to me? A year and half together shouldn't end like this—after all that I have done for him.* Then her anger turned inward, and destructive self-talk, attacks and accusations from the enemy began to assault her. *You're worthless. You can't do anything right. No one will ever love you, especially not now—you're used goods. You call yourself a Christian? You're just a little tramp. No man will ever love you.*

Over the next few weeks, Jan started to spend more and more time alone. She didn't want to see her friends; they would just ask about Chad. It seemed like her room was the only safe place. So she started to drop out of school and activities such as volleyball and cheerleading. Her grades took a dive as well. The only thing she wanted to do was stay home in her room and escape in her music. She didn't want to eat. At first, when Chad broke up with her, she couldn't sleep; but now she would sleep all the time. She started to sleep in class and miss more and more school. When her parents began to get notes from the school about her poor grades and behavior, they tried to talk to her. Jan would listen to their concerns and promise to do better, but inside she just did not care. Her friends Ashley and Morgan became distant.

"Can you tell me what in the world is the matter with Jan?" asked Ashley.

"I don't know," said Morgan. "She seems like a totally different person!"

Jan was experiencing depression. At one time, depression was thought to be only an adult problem, but now we understand that depression affects many teens and preteens. Researchers even concede that depression frequently occurs in children.[1] Josh McDowell reported "nearly 5 percent of all teens are identified as clinically depressed every year."[2]

What do people mean when they say they are depressed? Well, some use the word "depression" just to relate sadness, or the blues. But depression is much more. Let's start with a good dictionary definition.

Merriam-Webster's Collegiate Dictionary defines depression as "a state of feeling sad" but adds a second definition: "a psychoneurotic or psychotic disorder marked especially by sadness, inactivity, difficulty in thinking and concentration, a significant increase or decrease in appetite and time spent sleeping, feelings of dejection and hopelessness, and sometimes suicidal tendencies."[3]

Sometimes teens who struggle with depression do not believe that anyone can relate to their circumstances or understand what they are going through. Their reasoning goes something like this: If no one else understands, then how can God understand? After all, if God does not like the circumstances, He can create new ones. He does not have to deal with our finite limitations; He is eternal and infinite. He has no impure thoughts, nor does He struggle against insurmountable odds.

JESUS CAN RELATE

All of this is wonderfully true of our heavenly Father, but remember Jesus' circumstances. Jesus humbled Himself and took on the form of a man (see Phil. 2:6-8). He voluntarily surrendered the independent use of His divine attributes. All of the political and religious forces of His day were united against Him. In the end, He was alone. His chosen disciples deserted Him. Peter even denied that he knew Jesus. In the garden of Gethsemane, Jesus was grieved and distressed to the point of death. He became the Man of Sorrows, acquainted with grief. Finally, He faced the indignities of a mock trial and was found guilty of trumped-up charges. The most innocent Man who ever lived was crucified. According to Hebrews 4:14-16, because of Jesus, we can go to God when we are struggling or depressed:

> Since then we have a great high priest who has passed through the heavens, Jesus the Son of God, let us hold fast our confession. For we do not have a high priest who cannot sympathize with our weaknesses, but one who has been tempted in all things as we are, yet without sin. Let us therefore draw near with confidence to the throne of grace, that we may receive mercy and may find grace to help in time of need.

Jesus made it possible for us to go to God, not only because He died for our sins and gave us eternal life, but also because He, by His own experience, can relate to our weaknesses. He knows from personal experience how we feel.

Have you ever felt rejected and unloved? So has He. Have people you counted on ever let you down? People let Him down, too. Do you face overwhelming temptation? He was tempted in *all* ways. Do you have to live with the consequences of someone else's sins? He took upon Himself the sins of *all* mankind and then faced what you and I will never have to face: the Father turned His back on Him.

Yet, in the end, God did not abandon His Son. And we can say with confidence that He will never leave us or forsake us (see Heb.

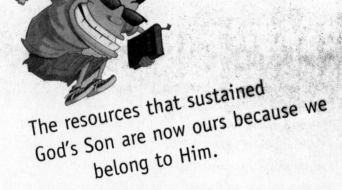

The resources that sustained God's Son are now ours because we belong to Him.

13:5). In spite of all that Christ endured, He never lost hope or faith in our heavenly Father. The resources that sustained God's Son are now ours because we belong to Him. He is the God of all hope.

CRYING FOR MERCY AND NEEDING GRACE

We have the assurance that if we go to God, we will receive mercy and find grace to help us in times of need. He will not give us what we deserve (which demonstrates His mercy); instead, He will give us what we need (which demonstrates His grace).

Young people often turn to a Christian youth group or the Church when they are hurting and in trouble. Yet they do not always find mercy there. In too many cases, they receive more mercy and less judgment in a secular treatment center or from their unsaved friends. However, these mainstream resources cannot offer the eternal grace of God—only the Church has the

grace to help in times of need. But we will not have the opportunity to share it unless we first show mercy.

The cry of a depressed teen is "Have mercy on me. I don't
need to be scolded, judged, advised or rejected. I need to be
understood, accepted, affirmed and loved." If what the teen
needs does not come first, then all the biblical answers we have
to give him will fall upon deaf ears.

HIDING IN THE SHADOWS

Teenage or adolescent depression, as opposed to that experienced and displayed by adults, can be even more difficult to cat-
egorize and identify. Dr. Ross Campbell writes:

> Teenage depression is difficult to identify because its
> symptoms are different from the classical symptoms of
> adult depression. For example, a teenager in mild
> depression acts and talks normally. There are no out-
> ward signs of depression. Mild teenage depression is
> detectable only by somehow knowing the child's
> thought pattern and thought content. Few professionals
> even can pick up depression in this state.
>
> In moderate depression, also, the teenager acts and
> talks normally. However, in moderate depression, the
> content of the teenager's speech is affected, dwelling pri-
> marily on depressing subjects such as death, morbid
> problems, and crises. Since many adults today seem to
> dwell on pessimistic trains of thought, the teenager's
> depression may go unnoticed . . .
>
> In the vast majority of cases, only in severe depression
> does the teenager actually appear depressed. . . . There is an
> exception to this, however. Teenage depression is difficult

to identify because teens are good at "masking" it; that is, they can cover it by appearing OK even when they are absolutely miserable. This is often called *smiling depression*. This is a front that teenagers employ unconsciously . . . primarily when other people are around. When depressed teenagers are alone, they let down or relax the mask somewhat.

This is helpful to parents. If we are able to see our teenagers at times when they believe no one is looking at them, we may be able to identify depression.[4]

Simply determining the causes and cures of depression presents a challenge because the symptoms reveal that the whole person is affected—body, soul and spirit. We know that many people become physically sick for mental, emotional or spiritual reasons.[5] It is also known that many people who suffer from emotional problems can establish a physical cause. Humanly speaking, people often find themselves hoping that a physical cause and cure can be found for depression, because there is less of a social stigma associated with physical illness than there is with mental illness. Somehow we feel absolved of responsibility if a physical cause can be established. Our self-image is left intact. We believe other people will be more sympathetic if they know our physical condition is not our fault.

With that kind of thinking, people are afraid to share their real problems. Tremendous needs go unmet when people will disclose their physical problems, but not their emotional or spiritual ones. Generally speaking, the Christian community does not respond appropriately to people who struggle with their emotions. On the other hand, if a friend breaks her leg, we flock to the hospital, pray for her and sign her cast. Meals are brought over to her house. She is treated almost like a hero, because people understand physical frailties and they can sympathize.

Compare this to what happens in a youth group when a prayer request is given for someone who is depressed. A gloom hangs over the room, and a polite prayer is offered. "Dear Lord, help Jan get over her depression. Amen." We do not know how to respond to emotional problems. There is no cast to sign, and everyone is silently thinking (or the depressed person believes that others are thinking), *Why doesn't she just snap out of it? I wonder what skeletons she has in her closet. If she would just pray and read her Bible more, she wouldn't be in such a state. No sincere Christian should be depressed. There must be some sin in her life.* These critical thoughts do not help the depressed person and often are not even true. Contributing to the person's guilt and shame does not help his or her mental functioning. We must learn to reflect the love and hope of God, who is close to the brokenhearted.

TWO KINDS OF DEPRESSION

REACTIVE DEPRESSION:
A RESPONSE TO SOMETHING OUTSIDE THE BODY

ENDOGENOUS DEPRESSION:
COMES FROM WITHIN THE BODY OR IS PHYSICAL IN ITS ORIGIN

Is there a physical cause, and therefore a potential physical cure, for some forms of depression? Yes, and we will examine these possibilities. Christians are no more immune to either form of depression than any other person. Therefore, it is wrong to jump to the conclusion that it is a sin for a Christian to be depressed.

We have a far greater hope for cure, however, if the cause of our depression is *not* endogenous but reactive—a response to something outside the body. This is because changing brain chemistry is far less certain and less precise than changing what we believe or how we think about external circumstances or events. However, it is usually easier to get people to take a pill with the hope of changing brain chemistry than to get them to change what they believe and how they think.

People who are depressed because of the way they think and believe are often shunned or judged. But what about those people whose thinking makes them arrogant, prideful and self-sufficient? The depressed person would find a more kindred spirit with the biblical prophets, who thundered against such arrogance, than they find in many youth groups.

SEEKING A WHOLE ANSWER

In one sense, it does not make any difference whether the primary cause of depression is physical, mental or spiritual. Depression affects the whole person, and a complete cure requires a holistic answer. No human problem that manifests itself in one dimension of reality can be isolated from the rest of reality. Like any other sickness of the body and soul, depression is a whole-life problem that requires a whole-life answer.

Depression is related to our physical health, to what we believe, how we perceive ourselves, our relationship with God, our relationship with others, the circumstances of our lives and, finally, to Satan, the god of this world. We cannot successfully treat depression without taking into account all of these related factors. We have a whole God, the Creator of all reality, and He relates to us as whole people.

WE ARE IN THIS TOGETHER

It is not shameful to feel depressed, because some measure of depression is an inevitable part of our maturing process. About 10 percent of all adults will suffer from depression in any given year, according to the National Institute of Health. Only a third of those people will seek treatment. It is estimated that 10 percent of all children in this country suffer from some form of depression before they reach the age of 12. As many as 20 percent of all school-age children (including teens) suffer from some form of depression. Our children are at risk of being more than simply down in the dumps. Teen depression has reached epidemic proportions.[6]

In too may cases, pride prevents the depressed person, his family and his friends from seeking proper help, and the consequences are often predictable and tragic. As the Bible declares, pride comes before a fall, and God is opposed to the proud (see Prov. 16:18).

It is more honest to admit that we need help than to pretend we can live the Christian life alone. Our drive to be self-sufficient destroys our dependency on Christ. Only those who are secure in Christ will readily admit to their need for one another, and they do not hesitate to ask for help when it becomes necessary. We absolutely need God, and we desperately need each other. It is the essence of love to meet each other's needs.

King David was said to have a heart for God, yet his numerous bouts of depression are recorded throughout the psalms. Martin Luther battled depression most of his life. Abraham Lincoln said, "I am now the most miserable man living. If what I feel were equally distributed to the whole human family, there would not be one cheerful face on the earth."[7]

Let's face it: Living in this fallen world can be quite depressing. But there are benefits to acknowledging all of our struggles.

Christian growth can come from times of loss and feelings of helplessness or hopelessness. The richest treasures are often discovered in the deepest holes. What we need is the assurance that can only come from a God of all hope. It has been said, "We can live about 40 days without food, about three days without water and about eight minutes without air—but only one second without hope."

RESTORING HOPE

Depression is as serious as any other illness or accident. Depression can steal our hope and get us to question our true identity as believers. Yet in the middle of our hopelessness stands Jesus. He is there to point us to the Father and His inspiration. Jesus shows us how to see things through the Father's eyes. Lonni Collins Pratt tells how this happened to her:

> I saw the car just before it hit me. I seemed to float. Then darkness smashed my senses.
>
> I came to in an ambulance. Opening my eyes, I could see only shreds of light through my bandaged, swollen eyelids. I didn't know it then, but small particles of gravel and dirt were embedded in my freckled sixteen-year-old face. As I tried to touch it, someone tenderly pressed my arm down and whispered, "Lie still."
>
> A wailing siren trailed distantly somewhere, and I slipped into unconsciousness. My last thoughts were a desperate prayer: "Dear God, not my face, please . . . "
>
> Like many teenage girls, I found much of my identity in my appearance. Adolescence revolved around my outside image. Being pretty meant I had lots of dates and a wide circle of friends.

My father doted on me. He had four sons, but only one daughter. I remember one Sunday in particular. As we got out of the car at church, my brothers—a scruffy threesome in corduroy and cowlicks—ran ahead. Mom had stayed home with the sick baby.

I was gathering my small purse, church school papers, and Bible. Dad opened the door. I looked up at him, convinced in my seven-year-old heart that he was more handsome and smelled better than any daddy anywhere.

He extended his hand to me with a twinkle in his eye and said, "A hand, my lady?" Then he swept me up into his arms and told me how pretty I was. "No father has ever loved a little girl more than I love you," he said.

In my child's heart, which did not really understand a father's love, I thought it was my pretty dress and face he loved.

A few weeks before the accident, I had won first place in a local pageant, making me the festival queen! Dad did not say much. He just stood beside me with his arm over my shoulders, beaming with pride. Once more, I was his pretty little girl. I basked in the warmth of his love and acceptance.

About this time, I made a personal commitment to Christ. In the midst of student council, honor society, pageants, and parades, I was beginning a relationship with God.

In the hours immediately after my accident, I drifted in and out of consciousness. Whenever my mind cleared even slightly, I wondered about my face. I was bleeding internally and had a severe concussion, but it never occurred to me that my concern with appearance was disproportionate.

The next morning, although I could not open my eyes more than a slit, I asked the nurse for a mirror. "You just concern yourself with getting well, young lady," she said, not looking at my face as she took my blood pressure.

Her refusal to give me a mirror, I reasoned, meant it must be worse that I imaged. My face felt tight and itchy. It burned and ached other times. I didn't touch it, though, because my doctor told me that might cause infection.

My parents also battled to keep mirrors away. As my body healed internally and strength returned, I became increasingly difficult.

At one point, for the fourth time in less than an hour, I pleaded for a mirror. Five days had passed since the accident.

Angry and beaten down, Dad snapped, "Don't ask again! I said no and that's it!"

I wish I could offer an excuse for what I said. I propped myself on my elbows, and through lips that barely moved, hissed, "You don't love me. Now that I'm not pretty anymore, you just don't love me!"

Dad looked as if someone had knocked the life out of him. He slumped into a chair and put his head in his hands. My mother walked over and put her hand on his shoulder as he tried to control tears. I collapsed against the pillows.

I didn't ask my parents for the mirror again. Instead, I waited until someone from housekeeping was straightening my room the next morning.

My curtain was drawn as if I was taking a sponge bath. "Could you get me a mirror, please?" I asked. "I must have mislaid mine." After a little searching, she found one and discreetly handed it to me around the curtain.

Nothing could have prepared me for what I saw. An image that resembled a giant scraped knee, oozing and bright pink, looked at me. My eyes and lips were crusted swollen. Hardly a patch of skin, ear-to-ear, had escaped the trauma.

My father arrived a little later with magazines and homework tucked under his arm. He found me staring into the mirror. Prying my fingers one by one from the mirror, he said, "It isn't important. This doesn't change anything that matters. No one will love you less."

Finally he pulled the mirror away and tossed it into a chair. He sat on the edge of my bed, took me into his arms, and held me for a long time.

"I know what you think," he said.

"You couldn't," I mumbled, turning away and staring out the window.

"You're wrong," he said, ignoring my self-pity.

"This will not change anything," he repeated. He put his hand on my arm, running it over an IV line. "The people who love you have seen you at your worst, you know."

"Right, seen me with rollers or with cold cream—not with my face ripped off!"

"Let's talk about me then," he said. "I love you. Nothing will ever change that because it is you I love, not your outside. I've changed your diapers and watched your skin blister with chicken pox. I've wiped up your bloody noses and held your head while you threw up in the toilet. I've loved you when you weren't pretty."

He hesitated. "Yesterday you were ugly—not because of your skin, but because you behaved ugly. But I'm here today, and I'll be here tomorrow. Fathers don't stop loving their children, no matter what life takes. You will be blessed if life only takes your face."

I turned to my father, feeling it was all words, the right words, spoken out of duty—polite lies.

"Look at me then, Daddy," I said. "Look at me and tell me you love me."

I will never forget what happened next. As he looked into my battered face, his eyes filled with tears. Slowly he leaned toward me, and with his eyes open, he gently kissed my scabbed, oozing lips.

It was the kiss that tucked me in every night of my young life, the kiss that warmed each morning.

Many years have passed. All that remains of my accident is a tiny indentation just above one eyebrow. But my father's kiss, and what it taught me about love, will never leave.[8]

If you have ever struggled with depression, we have written this book to help you establish your hope in God and enable you to live according to the truth of God's Word. We want to extend to you the mercy and grace of God. Depression, despair and hopelessness may have crept into your life and tainted your view of reality. Truth restores hope. We want to help you see the reality of the world we live in through the grid of Scripture. Wisdom is seeing life from God's perspective. We hope that this book will teach you about the Father's kiss.

In this book we hope to accomplish the following:

1. describe the signs of depression;
2. explain medical terms, to show how depression can have an impact on our bodies;
3. show how thinking and believing affect the way we respond to the world about us;
4. establish the spiritual connection between depression and mental health;

5. reveal the Father nature of God and how He relates to us;

6. explain the gospel and emphasize its message of who we are in Christ and what it means to be a child of God;

7. uncover the truth from Scripture that replaces our sense of hopelessness and helplessness;

8. show how to survive the inevitable losses of life and reinforce the truth that any crisis can be a stepping-stone to greater growth and maturity;

9. show how suffering is an essential part of becoming like Christ (sanctification);

10. provide a step-by-step process for overcoming depression.

Listen to how Jesus prays in His high priestly prayer: "But now I come to Thee; and these things I speak in the world, that they may have My joy made full in themselves" (John 17:13).

To think you are unloved, unappreciated and unworthy is to believe a lie, because you are a child of the King who has rescued you from the domain of darkness, and brought you to the kingdom of His beloved Son.

Paul writes, "Not that we lord it over your faith, but are workers with you for your joy; for in your faith you are standing firm" (2 Cor. 1:24).

God wants you to experience the joy of the Lord. It is a fruit of the Spirit (see Gal. 5:22), not the fruit of circumstances. We are coworkers for your joy. However, the Christian walk is not about trying to be happy; that would be trite, misguided and self-serving.

We are called to be mission-minded overcomers in Christ. We are not called to live lives that are continuously beaten down, defeated or in bondage. To see yourself as rejected, unwanted and useless is to be deceived. To see the circumstances of life as hopeless is to take your eyes off Jesus, the Author and Finisher of your faith. To think you are unloved, unappreciated and unworthy is to believe a lie, because you are a child of the King who has rescued you from the domain of darkness and brought you to the kingdom of His beloved Son (see Col. 1:13). God's love for you is unconditional because God *is* love. It is His nature to love you.

Our prayer is that you will sense our compassion and understanding derived from years of helping young people who have lost their hope. It is imperfect; but God's love and compassion are perfect, and He is your hope. We wanted to be hard-hitting enough to break down the mental strongholds of hopelessness and helplessness yet tender enough to bind up the brokenhearted. We believe the personal presence of Christ in your life and the truth of His Word are ultimately the answers. Our desire is to make that truth relevant to your struggles, as well as practical enough to inspire immediate action.

Now may the God of hope fill you with all joy and peace in believing, that you may abound in hope by the power of the Holy Spirit (Rom. 15:13).

DEPRESSION BUSTERS

Read:

Hebrews 4:14-16

Reflect:

1. How would you define depression?
2. Why do you think depression is so widespread today?
3. Have you ever felt rejected and unloved, or have you ever had people you counted on let you down? How can Jesus relate to these circumstances?
4. Why do you think so many people experience shame when they go through depression?

Respond:

Oh, Lord, in my hopelessness I cry out to You. I ask You now to hear me and to touch me and destroy the despair in my life and body. I pray that every enemy of the Lord Jesus Christ be removed from my presence, that I might hear only from You, Lord. I pray that You would fill me with hope, fill me with joy, fill me with peace. I pray that my belief and trust in You would spill over into my mind, my will and my emotions. Fill me with Your life-giving energy, the energy of the Holy Spirit, so I would brim over with hope. In Jesus name I pray. Amen.

Notes

1. Josh McDowell and Bob Hostetler, *Handbook on Counseling Youth* (Dallas: Word Publishing, 1996), p. 61.
2. Ibid.
3. Ibid.
4. Ibid., p. 62.
5. It is a well-established fact that some people become physically sick from mental, emotional and spiritual causes. It is estimated that between 50 percent and 75 percent of sick people become ill due to these causes. At least 25 percent of the healings in the Gospels are actually deliverance from evil spirits.
6. Walt Mueller, *Understanding Today's Youth Culture* (Wheaton, IL: Tyndale House Publishers, Inc., 1994), p. 296.
7. Abraham Lincoln, in a letter to his friend William Henry Herdon, quoted in Michael Burlingame, *The Inner World of Abraham Lincoln* (Urbana, IL: University of Illinois Press, 1994), p. 100.
8. Lonni Collins Pratt, "Through a Father's Eyes," *Moody Monthly* (September 1992).

CHAPTER 2

THE WORLD BELOW— THE AGONY OF DEPRESSION

The joy of the LORD is your strength.

NEHEMIAH 8:10

I have everything I need for joy!

ROBERT REED

"I have everything I need for joy!" Robert Reed said.

Amazing, I thought.

His hands are twisted and his feet are useless. He can't bathe himself. He can't feed himself. He can't brush his teeth, comb his hair or put on his underwear. His shirts are held together by strips of Velcro. His speech drags like a worn-out audiocassette.

Robert has cerebral palsy.

The disease keeps him from driving a car, riding a bike and going for a walk. But it didn't keep him from graduating from high school or attending Abilene Christian University, from which he graduated with a degree in Latin. Having cerebral palsy didn't keep him from teaching at a St. Louis junior college or from venturing overseas on five mission trips.

And Robert's disease did not prevent him from becoming a missionary in Portugal.

He moved to Lisbon, alone, in 1972. There he rented a hotel room and began studying Portuguese. He found a restaurant owner who would feed him after the rush hour and a tutor who would instruct him in the language.

Then he stationed himself daily in a park, where he distributed brochures about Christ. Within six years, he led seventy people to the Lord, one of whom became his wife, Rosa.

I heard Robert speak recently. I watched other men carry him in his wheelchair onto the platform. I watched them lay a Bible in his lap. I watched his stiff fingers force open the pages. And I watched people in the audience wipe away tears of admiration from their faces. Robert could have asked for sympathy or pity, but he did just the opposite. He held his bent hand up in the air and boasted, "I have everything I need for joy."

His shirts are held together by Velcro, but his life is held together by joy![1]

A SAD EPIDEMIC

How is it that some people are able to find joy in the darkest of circumstances and avoid the cold grip of depression while too many others seem unable to escape its icy grasp? How can we learn to hold our lives together with joy, even in the midst of great discouragement? The answers to these questions are what this book is all about.

Depression is an ache that starts in the soul and then crushes your spirit. It wraps itself so tightly around you that you cannot believe it will ever leave. But it can be controlled and it does depart! Depression is treatable. You do not have to live with it, at least not for long.

At this writing, about 10 million people in the United States are suffering from depression. It can creep into the lives of all people regardless of age, gender, education level, social ranking or economic status. Among college students, 25 percent struggle with some form of depression, and 33 percent of college dropouts suffer serious depression before leaving school. Fifty percent more girls experience depression than boys.

The number of doctor visits in which patients diagnosed with mental problems received prescriptions rose from 32.7 million to 45.6 million in the decade from 1985 to 1994. Visits to the doctor that resulted in a diagnosis of depression almost doubled during the same 10-year period, from 11 million to more than 20.4 million.[2] This is an incredible increase, especially in light of the fact that many who struggle with depression do not seek medical help.

Many people will have at least one serious bout of depression in their lifetime.

Depression is a complex yet common physical, emotional and spiritual struggle. It is so prevalent that it has been called the common cold of psychological disorders. Many people will have at least one serious bout of depression in their lifetime, and all will experience some symptoms of depression due to poor physical health, negative circumstances or weak spiritual condition.

Too many Christian teens live in denial about their own depression, thinking that if they were spiritually mature they would never have to struggle like others do. Consequently, they do not reach out to anyone or seek the help they need. It is actually shameful in some "Christian" communities to be sad or depressed. "You must be living in sin" is the subtle, deceptive assumption. That kind of thinking causes depressed teens to clam up and hide their true feelings instead of believing the truth and walking in the light.

DEFINITION OF DEPRESSION

Depression is a disturbance, or disorder, of a person's mood, or emotional state. It is characterized by persistent sadness, heaviness, darkness or feelings of emptiness. The emotional state of depression is usually accompanied by thoughts of hopelessness and sometimes suicide. Those who are depressed believe that life is bad and that the chances for improvement are nil. Their thoughts are colored by negative views of themselves, their future and the circumstances surrounding them.

It is critically important to realize that sadness or other factors in the *emotional state* of depression are not the cause but the symptom. Treating the symptom would only bring temporary relief at best. Any treatment for depression must focus on the cause, not the effect. The goal is to cure the disease, not the resulting pain. As we shall learn later, the cause could be physical, mental or spiritual. We think it is important to understand the symptoms of depression in order to better understand the cause. A proper diagnosis is necessary before appropriate treatment can be considered.

PHYSICAL SYMPTOMS OF DEPRESSION

While depression moves from spirit to soul, it also directly affects the body.

Energy Level

"I just don't feel like doing anything" is the song of the depressed. Loss of energy and never-ending tiredness are the characteristics of depression. People who suffer from depression live as though their internal transmission has only one gear—low—and they would prefer to shift into neutral.

A recurring song in the old television program *Hee Haw* captured the image of depression. A bunch of hillbillies are flaked out in front of an old cabin, clutching their moonshine, with a droopy bloodhound at their side. Each night they sing the theme song of the depressed:

Gloom, despair and agony on me;
Deep, dark depression, excessive misery;
If it weren't for bad luck,
I'd have no luck at all;
Gloom, despair and agony on me!

For those who suffer from depression, ordinary bodily movements and actions are reduced to slow motion. Walking, talking, cleaning a room, getting ready for school or doing a project can take considerably longer than usual. The student suffering from depression often feels that time is moving at a snail's pace. Everyday activities become monumental tasks or seemingly impossible to complete. Complaints of tiredness are common. Lowered energy levels and lessened interest in activities affect homework and grades. The student can often see that his or her study habits and performance are sliding, but the student cannot seem to pull out of the mire.

Approximately 10 percent of depressed students have serious struggles with endogenous depression, which, as explained earlier, originates within the body and is characterized by physical symptoms. Many of these teens simply do not function on a daily basis. They do not get dressed and either stay in bed or lie around the house.

Sleep Disturbance

Having trouble sleeping is one of the most common signs of depression. Although some teens feel like sleeping all the time when they become depressed, it is actually more common to suffer insomnia.

There are different kinds of insomnia. Initial insomnia, or sleep onset insomnia, is the difficulty of falling asleep. Depression is more commonly associated with terminal insomnia, during which the person falls asleep out of sheer fatigue but then wakes up and cannot get back to sleep. Although insomnia is only a symptom of depression, it contributes to the downward spiral of those who cannot seem to pull out of it. Inadequate sleep leaves the sufferer with a low energy level for the tasks of the next day.

Psalm 77 is a call for help by Asaph, who is so depressed that he cannot sleep. He writes, "When I remember God, then I am disturbed; when I sigh, then my spirit grows faint. Thou hast held my eyelids open; I am so troubled that I cannot speak" (vv. 3-4). This sufferer also questions God's mercy and compassion (see vv. 7-9). His hope is gone because what he believes about God is not true; and the result is sleeplessness, despair about God's seeming absence and not enough energy to even speak. That is depression.

Activity Level

Depression is accompanied by decreased involvement in activities such as sports and student clubs, which is related to an overall lack of interest, commitment and follow-through in day-to-day affairs. Sufferers do not have the physical or emotional energy to sustain ordinary levels of vigor, so their performance is often hindered. They lose interest in activities that they formerly found to be meaningful and fun.

Many teens find it difficult to pray because God seems like a distant figure. Perhaps they enjoyed playing the piano or some other instrument, but they no longer find it fun or satisfying. *Why bother?* is the question that screams for an answer! Tragically, the needs for self-expression and to be involved with others go unmet, which only contributes to the deepening of depression.

Isolation

A depressed person desires isolation, feels worthless, criticizes his personal appearance, loses spontaneity and becomes apathetic. The emotional state of depression usually creates problems in relationships. It is common to see young people who suffer with depression pull away from other people. They feel embarrassed to be with people when they feel so low. They do not want to be a wet blanket in the youth group or drag others down. They just want to be alone.

Although some may think that isolation is a viable short-term solution, avoiding people often adds to the downward spiral of depression.

Aches and Pains

When depression strikes, many people report physical aches and pains such as headaches, stomachaches and lower back pain. These ailments can be quite severe. Depression-caused headaches are common. Unlike migraine headaches, they are usually dull and feel like a band around the head with the pain radiating down the neck. These aches and pains associated with depression are not new: King David laments: "I am bowed down and brought very low; all day long I go about mourning. My back is filled with searing pain; there is no health in my body" (Ps. 38:6-7, *NIV*).

Loss of Appetite

Depression is often accompanied by a decrease in appetite. Indigestion, constipation or diarrhea can contribute to weight loss. People who struggle with anorexia and deny themselves adequate nourishment are usually depressed as well. On the other hand, 20 percent of depressed young people experience an increase of appetite and crave food.

MENTAL AND EMOTIONAL SYMPTOMS

Most symptoms of depression are emotional. Sometimes what the average person thinks can cause dejection and some mental problems can lead to mild and even serious depression. Some of the most common emotional symptoms and resultant mental states of depressed people are sadness, despair, irritability, negative thought patterns and thoughts of suicide.

Sadness

Depression is commonly characterized by a deep sadness. The blues seem to creep up slowly and bring with them a spirit of heaviness. Crying or just being in a funk are widespread among depressed teens. Some can hardly control the steady stream of tears. The sadness they experience is the opposite of joy, which is a fruit of the Spirit (see Gal. 5:22-23). Proverbs 15:13 reads, "A joyful heart makes a cheerful face, but when the heart is sad, the spirit is broken."

Despair

Despair is the absence of hope. It causes a person to see no light at the end of the tunnel, no prospects at the end of the day and no answers for the endless rounds of questions. Three times the psalmist cries out, "Why are you in despair, O my soul? And why have you become disturbed within me? Hope in God, for I shall again praise Him for the help of His presence" (Ps. 42:5; see also Ps. 42:11 and Ps. 43:5).

Hope, despair's opposite, is the present assurance of some future good; and the psalmist knew where his hope lay. The problem is that depression seems to mess up the normal process of memory.

Irritability

Depressed teens have very little emotional reserve. Small things tick them off, and they are easily frustrated. They have a low tolerance level for the pressures of life and can be frequently heard saying "I can't deal with that right now" or "I just can't take it any longer."

Negative Thought Patterns

Most often, depressed people have trouble thinking and concentrating. Their minds will not stay focused. Constant distractions rob them of any mental peace. Just as water seeks the lowest ground, depression likewise seeps in and drowns out everything else, including optimism. For a depressed person, it seems easier to see a problem, think the worst, predict failure, find fault and focus on weakness.

Teens who are prone to depression have difficulty believing positive and good things about themselves. Feelings of worthlessness become the breeding ground for thoughts of self-destruction.

They cannot think positively about the future. They cannot stop worrying about tomorrow. They dread it, instead of looking forward to it.

Depressed teens put a negative spin on the circumstances in which they find themselves.

Thoughts of Suicide

Sadness, isolation, loss of energy, strained relationships and physical problems mess up one's perspective of self and the future. As helplessness and hopelessness stir in the mind, many people begin to think of suicide as a way of escape. Others just wish they were dead or that God would take them home!

In short, depressed teens become self-absorbed. Mental exhaustion causes them to take the easy path, which is to think negatively about themselves. Such self-absorption makes thinking of others extremely difficult. The depressed person will avoid hearing any bad news or taking on any more responsibility. He or she feels overwhelmed. It is a syndrome filled with misery, shame, sadness and guilt.

Getting to know all the signs and symptoms of depression is important, but sometimes we can get overwhelmed by the reality that we are in fact experiencing depression. Here is a perspective that might help at this point in the book.

One day a father took his rich family and his son on a trip to the country with the firm purpose of showing him how the poor people can be. They spent a day and a night on the farm of a very poor family. When they got back from their trip, the father asked his son, "How was the trip?"

"Very good, Dad!"

"Did you see how the poor people can be?" the father asked.

"Yeah!"

"And what did you learn?"

The son answered, "I saw that we have a dog at home, and they have four. We have a pool that reaches to the middle of the garden, they have a creek that has no end. We have imported lamps in the garden, they have the stars. Our patio reaches to the front yard, they have the whole horizon."

When the little boy was finished, his father was speechless. His son added, "Thanks, Dad, for showing me how poor we are!"[3]

If we want to reach out to teens who struggle with depression, we must view them as people, not bundles of symptoms.

Depression can have one good quality: It can make us dependent on Christ—and true dependence on Christ brings a richness to life that few experience. So are you rich or poor?

It is not enough for Christians to merely be aware of the general symptoms of depression. If we want to reach out to those who struggle with depression, we must view them as people, not bundles of symptoms. We want to show them the riches that they have in Christ.

KING DAVID

See if you can find the signs of depression in King David's life as described in Psalm 38:3-18 (*NIV*):

Because of your wrath there is no health in my body; my bones have no soundness because of my sin. My guilt has overwhelmed me like a burden too heavy to bear. My wounds fester and are loathsome because of my sinful folly. I am bowed down and brought very low; all day long I go about mourning. My back is filled with searing pain; there is no health in my body. I am feeble and utterly crushed; I groan in anguish of heart. All my longings lie open before you, O Lord; my sighing is not hidden from you. My heart pounds, my strength fails me; even the light has gone from my eyes. My friends and companions avoid me because of my wounds; my neighbors stay far away. Those who seek my life set their traps, those who would harm me talk of my ruin; all day long they plot deception. I am like a deaf man, who cannot hear, like a mute, who cannot open his mouth; I have become like a man who does not hear, whose mouth can offer no reply. I wait for you, O LORD; you will answer, O Lord my God. For I said, "Do not let them gloat or exalt themselves over me when my foot slips." For I am about to fall, and my pain is ever with me. I confess my iniquity; I am troubled by my sin.

This passage reveals that David is depressed, even though he is a man with a whole heart for God. David would have been diagnosed with most depression symptoms. He describes in graphic detail his physical, spiritual and emotional pain. He even feels that he is near death. David knows that his only hope is God, as he cries out at the end of the psalm, "Come quickly to help me, O Lord my Savior" (v. 22).

DEPRESSION CHECKUP

Are you depressed? Do you know someone who may be? Try filling out the following questionnaire, which can serve as a rough evaluation and help determine whether the condition, if present at all, is mild or severe.

Circle the number on a scale of 1 to 5 that best describes you (or the person you are evaluating). For example, on line 1, circle number 1 if you are exhausted all the time and 5 if you are a high-energy person. Circle 3 if you are generally somewhere in between, having neither high nor low energy. If you are applying this inventory to yourself, you will get a more accurate picture of your general condition if you take it when you are not reacting to a crisis. Some mild depressions are reactions to temporary setbacks or disheartening circumstances that may only last for a few hours or days. It is best to wait a few hours or days after such episodes before taking the inventory because they can momentarily skew the results.

1. Low energy   1 2 3 4 5   High energy

2. Difficulty sleeping   1 2 3 4 5   Uninterrupted
   or sleep all the time   sleeping patterns

3. No desire to be   1 2 3 4 5   Very involved
   involved in activities   in activities

4. Aches and pains   1 2 3 4 5   Feel great

5. Loss of appetite   1 2 3 4 5   Enjoy eating

6. Sad   1 2 3 4 5   Joyful

7. Despairing and   1 2 3 4 5   Hopeful and
   hopeless   confident

8. Irritable (low   1 2 3 4 5   Pleasant (high
   frustration tolerance)   frustration
                                              tolerance)

9. Withdrawn   1 2 3 4 5   Involved

10. Mental anguish   1 2 3 4 5   Peace of mind

11. Low sense   1 2 3 4 5   High sense
    of self-worth   of self-worth

12. Pessimistic   1 2 3 4 5   Optimistic (about
    (about the future)   the future)

13. Negative (perceive   1 2 3 4 5   Positive (Perceive
    most circumstances   most circum-
    as negative or even   stances as positive
    harmful)   and as opportuni-
                                              ties for growth)

14. Self-destructive   1 2 3 4 5   Self-preserving
    ("I and others would be   ("Glad I'm here.")
    better off if I weren't here.")

If you most often circled numbers 3 through 5, you are not struggling with depression. Most of the fluctuations on the right side of the scale can be explained by general health, differing temperaments and growing levels of maturity. A person of average health and maturity, having an introspective or generally pessimistic temperament, would likely circle many 3s and not be depressed. A young person of good health and maturity with an optimistic and outgoing personality would likely circle 4s and 5s.

Temperament and personality can affect many of the individual items on the inventory. You can get a rough determination of your level of depression if you add up all the circled numbers and compare them with the following ratings:

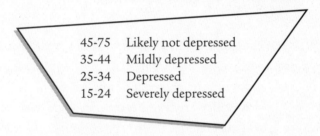

45-75   Likely not depressed
35-44   Mildly depressed
25-34   Depressed
15-24   Severely depressed

DEGREES OF DEPRESSION

Degrees of depression can range from mild to severe. Everyone experiences mild depression from time to time because of the normal ups and downs of life. These mood fluctuations are generally related to health issues, mental attitudes and the external pressures of living in a fallen world. In our experience, those who scored between 30 and 45 can manage their own recovery—and hopefully this book will help them do just that.

Those who score 29 or lower should seek the help of a godly pastor, youth pastor or Christ-centered counselor or if the cause is found to be endogenous or physical, see a medical doctor. Those who score low on the inventory need the objectivity of someone else to help them resolve their conflicts.

Please keep in mind that it is not a sign of failure or weakness to seek the help of others. We are supposed to "bear one

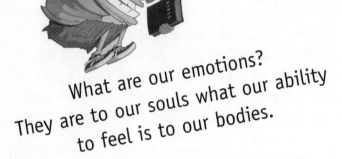

What are our emotions?
They are to our souls what our ability
to feel is to our bodies.

another's burdens, and thus fulfill the law of Christ" (Gal. 6:2). Every person needs God, and we need each other. Usually it is a sign of pride and immaturity to not admit a need.

Have you ever noticed that few people struggle with seeing a medical doctor if they are sick? But for some reason, we resist seeking help for emotional and spiritual problems. In our observation, people who are secure in Christ have no problem admitting their weaknesses. They are emotionally honest, as Jesus was when He wept over the city of Jerusalem and at the grave of Lazarus. He willingly and honestly admitted His need for emotional support when He cried out in the garden of Gethsemane, "My soul is deeply grieved to the point of death; remain here and keep watch" (Mark 14:34).

A WARNING SIGNAL

What are our emotions? They are to our souls what our ability to feel is to our bodies. Suppose someone had the power to remove the sensation of pain and offered it to you as a gift. Would you accept it? It sounds tempting, but if you could not feel pain, your body would be a hopeless mass of scars within weeks. The ability to feel pain is your protection from the harmful elements of the world we live in. Depression is a pain in the soul signaling that something is wrong.

Think of emotional pain as an indicator light on the control panel of a car. When that light comes on, you have three possible responses.

Suppression: Ignoring the Warning

You can ignore the warning signal and put a piece of duct tape over it. You may even be able to convince yourself for a while that the light is not on. That is called suppression, and in the long run it is very unhealthy. It is also dishonest when the cover-up is intended to convince others that everything is okay.

Let It All Hang Out: Breaking the Signal

Another option is to take a small hammer and break the light. When applied to our emotions, this is called indiscriminate expression, or "letting it all hang out." It may feel good for *you* to wear your emotions on your sleeves, but if you express them without discrimination, it is not healthy for others.

The Bible has a lot to say about being slow to speak and slow to anger (e.g., see Jas. 1:19). Be cautious about getting something off your chest at random or letting your feelings be known to all. Such displays will never bring the desired result. In suppression, the hurting person pulls away. In indiscriminate expression, others pull away.

Acknowledgment: Discovering the Cause

The third option is to look under the hood and seek to discover the cause. That is acknowledgment. In other words, be honest about how you feel for the purpose of resolving conflicts and living in harmony with God and His creation. This book is an attempt to look under the hood to discover the causes and cures of depression and to gain God's perspective, like the story of the two boxes.

> I have in my hands two boxes
> Which God gave me to hold.
> He said, "Put all your sorrows in the black,
> And all your joys in the gold."
> I heeded His words, and in the two boxes
> Both my joys and sorrows I store
> But though the gold became heavier each day
> The black was as light as before.
> With curiosity, I opened the black
> I wanted to find out why.
> And I saw, in the base of the box, a hole
> Which my sorrows had fallen out by,
> I showed the hole to God, and mused aloud,
> "I wonder where my sorrows could be."
> He smiled a gentle smile at me,
> "My child, they're all here with me."
> I asked, "God, why give me the boxes,
> Why the gold, and the black with the hole?"
> "My child, the gold is for you to count your
>   blessings,
> The black is for you to let go."[4]

We hope this book not only helps you let go of depression and hang on to the blessing but also nudges you to look under the hood and see why the warning lights are on. Only then can the root causes of depression be overcome by the truths of God.

DEPRESSION BUSTERS

Read:

Psalm 38:3-18

Reflect:

1. List at least five signs of depression.
2. If someone had the power to remove the sensation of pain and offered it to you as a gift, would you accept it? Why or why not?
3. What are the three possible responses we can have to emotional pain?
4. Why is letting all of your emotions out in one big burst not a very good idea?
5. Make a list of the signs of depression from the life of King David from Psalm 38:3-18.
6. Why do you think so many Christians have a hard time asking for help when they are depressed?

Respond:

Oh Lord, I want to be honest with You and honest with myself. Please reveal to me if I am struggling with depression. Help me, Lord, not to overrate my emotional state nor underrate it, but rather face the truth about my feelings and emotions. I choose not to ignore Your warning signal nor suppress my problems. And I choose not to coverup my depression and convince others that everything is okay. I also choose to be cautious about getting something off my chest at random or letting my feelings be known to all. Rather, Lord, I want to know the true source of my troubles, and I put my trust in You to show me that truth.

In Jesus' name I pray. Amen.

Notes

1. Alice Gray, comp., *Stories for the Extreme Teen's Heart* (Sisters, OR: Multnomah Publishers, 2000), pp. 158-159.
2. *The Denver Post*, February 18, 1998, p. 106.
3. Gray, *Stories*, p. 153.
4. Ibid., p. 254.

CHAPTER 3

No End In Sight– The Agony of the Body

I urge you therefore, brethren, by the mercies of God, to present your bodies a living and holy sacrifice, acceptable to God, which is your spiritual service of worship.

ROMANS 12:1

Trouble knocked at the door but, hearing laughter, hurried away.

BEN FRANKLIN

If you talk about skateboarding, then you need to speak the language. You have to know that an "ollie" is a skateboard trick and that a "half pipe" is a kind of ramp. You can ride a skateboard without knowing any jargon, but it is unlikely you will become very good and you will not know what other skaters are talking about. In the same way, if you want to understand your depression and how to overcome it, you will need to learn some new buzzwords.

Admittedly, reading the medical terms in this chapter will not be as much fun as doing an ollie on a half pipe, but it is necessary for you to understand the physical side of depression. These are the nuts and bolts. At times this chapter might seem a little technical, but hang in there. Take it slow. If you need to, look up some terms in a dictionary.

THE WHOLE PICTURE

When we start to deal with the brain and the chemical functions of our bodies, it is easy to forget that there is a hurting and confused human being involved. It is important that we realize that we are not just a bundle of chemical reactions but rather, children of God who are created in His awesome image. When we hear that someone is suffering from depression, we often stay away from that person as if he has some kind of contagious disease. But we really should show love and compassion. Do you remember the story of the good Samaritan? In Luke 10:25-37 (*THE MESSAGE*), Jesus tells this parable:

> Just then a religious scholar stood up with a question to test Jesus. "Teacher, what do I need to do to get eternal life?"
>
> He answered, "What's written in God's law? How do you interpret it?"

He said, "That you love the Lord your God with all your passion and prayer and muscle and intelligence—and that you love your neighbor as well as you do yourself."

"Good answer!" said Jesus. "Do it and you'll live."

Looking for a loophole, he asked, "And just how would you define 'neighbor'?"

Jesus answered by telling a story. "There was once a man traveling from Jerusalem to Jericho. On the way he was attacked by robbers. They took his clothes, beat him up, and went off leaving him half-dead. Luckily, a priest was on his way down the same road, but when he saw him he angled across to the other side. Then a Levite religious man showed up; he also avoided the injured man.

"A Samaritan traveling the road came on him. When he saw the man's condition, his heart went out to him. He gave him first aid, disinfecting and bandaging his wounds. Then he lifted him on to his donkey, led him to an inn, and made him comfortable. In the morning he took out two silver coins and gave them to the innkeeper, saying, 'Take good care of him. If it costs any more, put it on my bill—I'll pay you on my way back.'"

"What do you think? Which of the three became a neighbor to the man attacked by robbers?"

"The one who treated him kindly," the religion scholar responded.

Jesus said, "Go and do the same."

We truly love God when we love each other. This next story illustrates how easy it is to miss the mark and overlook those around us who are hurting.

Finals week had arrived with all its stress. I had been up late cramming for an exam. Now, as I slumped in my seat,

I felt like a spring that had been wound too tight. I had two tests back-to-back, and I was anxious to get through with them. At the same time I expected to be able to maintain my straight-A grade-point average.

As I waited impatiently for the professor to arrive, a stranger walked up to the blackboard and began to write:

"Due to a conflict, your professor is unable to give you your test in this classroom. He is waiting for you in the gymnasium."

Oh, great, I thought. *Now I have to walk clear across campus just to take this stupid exam.*

The entire class was scurrying out the door and rushing to the gym. No one wanted to be late for the final, and we weren't wasting time talking.

The route to the gym took us past the hospital. There was a man stumbling around in front of it. I recognized him as the young blind man whose wife had just given birth to a baby in that hospital. He had been there before, but he must have become confused.

Oh, well, I told myself. *Someone will come along soon and help him. I just don't have time to stop now.*

So I hurried along with the rest of the class on our way to take that final exam.

As we continued down the sidewalk, a woman came rushing out of a nearby bookstore.

She had a baby on one arm, a stack of books on the other, and a worried look on her face. The books fell onto the sidewalk, and the baby began to cry as she stooped to pick them up.

She should have left that kid at home, I thought. I dodged her as the class and I rushed along.

Just around the next corner someone had left a dog on a leash tied to a tree. He was a big, friendly mutt, and we had all seen him there before, but today he couldn't quite reach the pan of water left for him. He was straining at his leash and whining.

I thought, *What cruel pet owner would tie up a dog and not leave his water where he could reach it?* But I hurried on.

As we neared the gym, a car passed us and parked close to the door. I recognized the man who got out as one of the maintenance crew. I also noticed he left the lights on.

"He's going to have a problem when he tries to start that car to go home tonight," the fellow next to me said.

The professor stood with his arms folded, looking at us. We looked back. The silence became uncomfortable. We all knew his tests were also teaching tools, and we wondered what he was up to. He motioned toward the door, and in walked the blind man, the young mother with her baby, a girl holding the big dog on a leash, and the maintenance man.

These people had been planted along the way in an effort to test whether or not the class had grasped the meaning behind the story of the Good Samaritan and the man who fell among thieves. *We all failed.*[1]

Treating people kindly, loving them even when they are grouchy, cold and weird, is what Jesus was talking about in the story He told to the religious scholar.

A NEW AGE

We live in an incredible age. Some people say that knowledge doubles every two-and-a-half years and that junior high students have learned more in their few years than Benjamin Franklin did in his whole life.

Scientists and medical doctors know far more about the brain and how we function than ever before. Then why has the number of people seeking treatment for depression nearly doubled in the last 10 years? Is there a physical explanation for depression? Has our hope shifted from God to science? Professing ourselves to be wise, have we become fools? "For the foolishness of God is wiser than man's wisdom, and the weakness of God is stronger than man's strength" (1 Cor. 1:25, *NIV*). Or are we asked to make a false either/or choice? It should be both/and—utilizing both the wisdom of God and all the discoveries He has enabled humans to make.

A Collision Course?

We do not believe that science and the Bible are on a collision course. God is the Creator of all things, and He established the fixed order of the universe. "The heavens are telling of the glory of God; and their expanse is declaring the work of His hands" (Ps. 19:1). God is the author of science. We are a part of the creation, not the Creator. The fact that God has revealed Himself in creation is usually referred to as general revelation.

We can only make scientific discoveries through visual human research. How we interpret the data we observe from general revelation must be analyzed through the grid of special revelation, which is God's Word. A 50-year-old science textbook reads more like a comic book today. Who can predict what scientists will say 50 years from now about our present understanding of scientific discoveries?

Our confidence must be in God, but our faith in Him does not set us on a collision course with medical science. Advances in research do not disable or even diminish the power of God, nor do they collide with the revelation of His Word. We thank God for advancements in medicine that help reduce human suffering.

A 50-year-old science book reads more like a comic book today. Who can predict what scientists will say 50 years from now about our present understanding of scientific discoveries?

INNER AND OUTER ASPECTS

God created us in His image to be spiritually and physically alive. He formed Adam from the dust of the earth and breathed life into him. We have an outer person and an inner person, a material body and an immaterial soul.

God created the Church to minister to the soul and the spirit through the proper functioning of each member's gifts, talents and intelligence. Based on general revelation, humankind developed medical models to cure the physical body. However, because we are physical as well as spiritual beings, we need both the Church and the hospital, in a proper balance.

The material, or physical, part of humans relates to the external world through five senses. We can taste, smell, hear, feel and see. The inner person relates to God through the soul and spirit. Unlike the animal kingdom, which operates out of instinct, we have the capacity to think, feel and choose. Because we are "fearfully and wonderfully made" (Ps. 139:14), it would only make sense that God would create the outer person to work together with the inner person. Please refer to the following diagram:

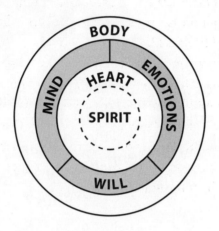

THE MIND-BRAIN CORRELATION

The correlation between the mind and the brain is obvious, but there is a big difference between the two. The brain came from the dust of this Earth and will return to dust when we die. At that moment we will be absent from our bodies and present with the Lord (see 2 Cor. 5:6-8), but we will not be mindless.

To illustrate the working relationship between the brain and the mind, picture a personal computer. Between our ears is a very powerful piece of equipment. Like a computer system, it comprises two distinct parts, the hardware and the software. The hardware—the computer itself—is obviously the brain.

The brain functions much like a digital computer that has millions of switching transistors that code all the information in a binary numbering system of 0s and 1s. The miniaturization of circuitry has made it possible to store and compile an incredible amount of information in a computer the size of a notebook. However, humankind has not even come close to making a computer as awesome as the one that is now making it possible for you to read and understand this book. A computer is mechanical, but our brains are living organisms composed of approximately 100 billion neurons. Each neuron is a living organism that in and of itself is like a microcomputer.

Pretend that you are back at school in your biology class. Do not panic—you will not be tested on this material! A basic anatomy lesson should be given at this point because we will refer to different parts of the body as we discuss possible causes and cures for physical depression. Every neuron is composed of a brain cell, an axon and many dendrites (inputs to the brain cell), as shown in the following illustration:

NEURONS

Each brain cell has many inputs (dendrites) and only one output through the axon that channels neurotransmitters to other dendrites. The axon has a covering known as the myelin sheath

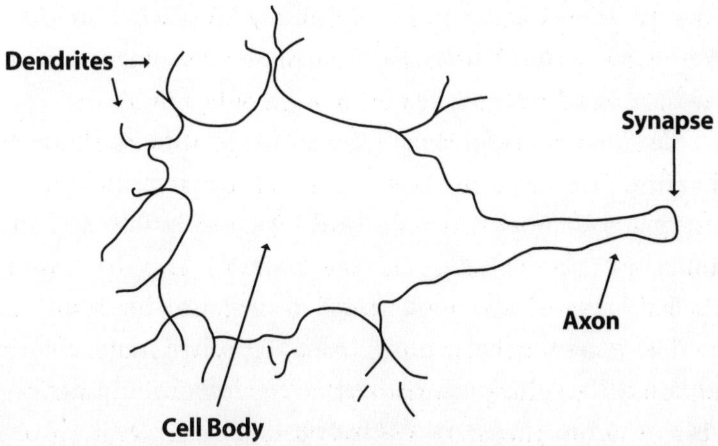

Dendrites →

Synapse

Axon

Cell Body

for insulation, because the cell sends electrochemical messages along the axon. Every neuron is connected to tens of thousands of other neurons. Given that there are 100 billion neurons, the potential number of combinations is mind-boggling.

A junction between the axon of one neuron and the dendrites of another is called a synapse. Through its dendrites, every brain cell receives information, which it processes, puts together and sends on to other neurons.

In the axon exist many mitochondria that produce neurotransmitters. When a signal from the cell reaches the axon, it releases neurotransmitters across the synapse to other dendrites.

BIPOLAR DEPRESSION

Physical depression is categorized as either bipolar or unipolar. A bipolar, or manic-depressive, illness has two poles: highs (manic moods) and lows (depressed moods). The manic symptoms include the following: increased energy, unrealistic and grandiose beliefs in one's own power and ability, wandering ideas and thoughts, poor judgment, increased talking or social activity, extreme happiness, irritability and distractibility, insensitive or irritating behavior, and abuse of alcohol or drugs. Extremely fearful, delusional and psychotic thinking is also possible during the manic phase.

Physical depression may have nothing to do with external circumstances. This may be an internal or physical struggle due to a chemical imbalance in the brain or possibly a battle for the mind.

The transmission of a message through the brain cells requires a certain balance of sodium (positive) and chloride (negative) ions. In bipolar illnesses, the abnormal polarity of positive and negative ions is out of balance.

UNIPOLAR DEPRESSION

Episodes of serious depression without corresponding highs often indicate unipolar depression. Depression of this type affects nearly 10 percent of the American population and appears to be increasing.

HELP FROM BOTH SIDES

The temptation among many young people is to believe that depression is purely a physical disorder requiring medical attention. That would be incorrect. Depression is a condition that affects the body, the soul and the spirit. If all three are linked to depression, then all three must also be avenues for a cure. Physical assessment or a medical exam is often needed when depression is moderate or severe.

Marcia struggled with extreme tiredness and felt incapable of doing even routine things at home. She could not eat and was not sleeping more than a few hours a night. Later, she wrote this letter describing what she went through.

The temptation among many young people is to believe that depression is purely a physical disorder requiring medical attention.

When I am in my depression, I feel like there is no hope. I
see no way out. I sit in my chair or on the couch and I can't
do much of anything. When I am depressed, everything
seems so overwhelming. It is even hard for me to eat. My
mind and body are weak. I feel this is the way it's going to
be forever. I want to wake up in the morning for once and
not dread the day, knowing it will be filled with fear and
hopelessness. No, I want to wake up and feel joy. The only
thing I could do was to cry out to God. In those times
when things felt the darkest, that's when God would
speak to me. He always seemed to bring scripture to me.

Marcia discovered through Christian counseling that truth
could indeed set her free, but she was also helped by seeing a
doctor who examined her physically. An antidepressant medication was prescribed to improve her concentration. This helped
her deal with issues in her life that needed to be resolved. Even
though doctors readily admit to a low degree of precision, medication is still accepted as a primary way of treating depression.
Prozac has been prescribed for more than 17 million Americans.
As of this writing, 580,000 teens and preteens are on the drug—
which now comes in peppermint flavor.

TOWARD A COMPLETE SOLUTION

If you were to stop reading at this point, you could easily conclude that depression can be cured simply by taking the right
medications. That kind of thinking would be unfortunate and
very wrong. We have helped many teens resolve their conflicts
and find their freedom in Christ without medication, but we
have seen few, if any, find total resolution of personal and inter-
personal conflicts by using medications alone. Only truth can
set a person free.

Medication cannot change circumstances or resolve personal and spiritual conflicts, but they can fix the computer in our heads, so the proper program can run. Similarly, it is hard to pray and read the Bible when we have the flu.

The fact that medications help depressed people feel better is not arguable—they do. But that is not the whole picture. After having been on an antidepressant medication for almost three weeks, one girl declared, "I didn't know the promises in the Bible were true for me until now." A proper use of medication enabled her to assume a responsible course of action!

Now check out this awesome testimony:

I am writing in regards to your seminar in Minnesota. The day it was to start, I was to be admitted to a hospital for the fifth time for manic depression. I have been dealing with this for almost two years. We had gone to several doctors and tried about every drug they could think of. I also had shock treatments. I attempted suicide twice. Unable to work any longer, I spent most of my days downstairs wishing I were dead or planning my next attempt. Also, it was a good place to protect myself from people and the world around me. I had a history of self-abuse. I have spent 30-odd years in jail or prisons. I was a drug addict and an alcoholic. I have been in drug and alcohol treatment 28 times.

I became a Christian several years ago but had always lived a defeated life. Now I was going back to the hospital to try new medications or more shock treatments. My wife and friends convinced me your seminar would be of more value. The hospital was concerned, because they believed I needed medical help. As the four days of the conference progressed, my head started to clear up! The Word of God was ministering to me, even though I was confused and in pain. I told one of your staff that I was in my eleventh hour. He set up an appointment for me.

The session lasted seven hours. They didn't leave one stone uncovered. The session was going great until I came to bitterness and unforgiveness. The three things that motivated my life were low self-esteem, anger and bitterness which were the result of being molested by a priest and suffering from many years of physical and verbal abuse in my childhood. I can honestly say I forgave them and God moved right in, lifting my depression. My eyes were now open to God's truth. I felt lighter than ever before. I did go to the hospital, but after two days they said I didn't need to be there. My doctors said I was a different person. They had never seen a person change so fast. They said, "Whatever you are doing, don't stop." I have been growing in the Lord daily. There is so much before Christ and after Christ that I could go on forever.

Non-Christian counselors seldom, if ever, see that kind of victory. Too many people continue in their depression because professionals with whom they have consulted have considered only one possible cause and therefore only one possible cure.

ONE-SIDED VIEWS

One Christian said, "My problem is just physical, and my doctor says I shouldn't let anyone tell me differently." She did admit that she had not found the right combination of drugs, but she had all the hope in the world that her doctor eventually would.

In the same church, another Christian said, "Taking drugs only shows a lack of faith." Of course, he had never experienced depression!

How could two people in the same church draw such different opinions? In our churches, we have observed the following four views that do not reflect a balanced Christian approach to helping depressed teens:

1. Taking medications shows a lack of trust in God.
2. Depression is a physical illness that can only be resolved by taking medications.
3. Depression is a spiritual attack and deliverance from demons is the only answer.
4. Depression is the guilt we feel as a result of unconfessed sin.

Such views are incomplete, wrong and not helpful for those who suffer from depression. We believe that God relates to us as whole people—body, soul and spirit. He sees us as people who live in a physical as well as a spiritual world.

FOCUSING ON THE SOFTWARE

We close this chapter by looking again at our computer illustration. If our brains represent the hardware, then our minds represent the software. The tendency of the Western world is to assume that mental or emotional problems are primarily caused by faulty hardware. There is no question that chemical imbalances take place. It would be a tragedy for a godly pastor or Christ-centered counselor to try helping a person who is physically sick without suggesting some medical attention. On the other hand, for a doctor to think that he can cure the whole person with medication alone is equally tragic. Taking a pill to heal the body is commendable, but taking a pill to mend the soul is wasteful. Fortunately, most doctors know that the medical model can take you only so far. Many in the medical profession acknowledge that a majority of their patients suffer for emotional *and* spiritual reasons.

Our view, however, is that in dealing with mental or emotional disorders the hardware is not the primary problem. We believe it is the software—the mental, emotional and spiritual parts of the whole person.

Other than submitting our bodies to God as living sacrifices and taking care of ourselves, we cannot do a lot to change the hardware; but we can totally change the software. How we think and what we choose to believe can actually change our biochemistry. In the next chapter, we will explore how this software, the mind, functions in relation to the rest of the body and in relation to the external world in which we live.

DEPRESSION BUSTERS

Read:

Romans 12:1-2

Reflect:

1. Why don't we believe that science and the Bible are on a collision course?
2. How does the brain function much like a digital computer?
3. What are bipolar and unipolar depression?
4. Why is medication only part of a possible solution for depression?

5. We have observed four views in our churches that do not reflect a balanced Christian approach to helping teens who are depressed. Can you list them and state why these views are harmful to people struggling with depression?

Respond:

Oh, Lord, I want to have balance in my life, so I am asking You to help me both physically and spiritually. Give me wisdom to seek both a doctor's care and a pastor's care. I want to see that my mind, body and spirit are healthy. Help me not to look just to medication for help but also to take responsibility for my spiritual life and resolve any spiritual issues that I might have with You or others. Lord, I know that You can and will help me. In Jesus' name I pray. Amen.

Note

1. Bernice Brookes, *Stuff You Don't Have to Pray About* (Nashville, TN: Broadman and Holman Publishers, 1995), n.p.

CHAPTER 4

FROZEN IN TIME–
THE AGONY OF
THE SOUL

For as he thinks within himself, so he is.

PROVERBS 23:7

*Have your heart right with Christ, and He will visit you often,
and so turn weekdays into Sundays, meals into sacraments,
homes into temples, and earth into heaven.*

CHARLES HADDON SPURGEON

I (Dave) was speaking at a conference in St. Cloud, Minnesota, to a crowd of about 1,400 young people. The room was filled with excitement, the worship band was playing, and the students were wound up and excited for the Lord. As I walked through the large room greeting people, one student in particular caught my eye. She was not sitting with the rest of the teens; rather, she was sitting on the floor, up against a side wall. She sat in a fetal position and wore a dark hat that covered most of her face. It was obvious that she was in a huge spiritual battle for her mind and that it was incredibly difficult for her to stay in the room with so much worship going on. I was drawn to her and as I stood over her, she was not even able to acknowledge my presence. Careful not to touch her or get too close, I softly said "I'm so glad you're here tonight. Do you mind if I pray for you, so you'll be able to hear what the Lord has for you?"

With a barely perceivable nod she shook her head yes. As a last ditch effort to bring hope back into her life, she had come to the conference with a youth worker she trusted. She was so deeply depressed that she could not carry on a tiny conversation. She had been dabbling in the occult, had been sexually involved with a number of people—including some same-sex relationships—and now her life was a fog of suicidal thoughts and depression. As I prayed for her, I asked that God would speak to her and surround her with His presence. I asked that He would allow her mind to be her own, a quiet place for just her and Him.

That night I spoke about our identity and freedom in Christ, and I introduced a tool to help resolve personal and spiritual conflicts called the Steps to Freedom in Christ. Before I could leave the hall, the girl with the dark hat came up to me with her youth pastor in tow. He stated that she wanted to resolve some stuff in her life and asked if she could go through the steps. I asked the girl, "Is that what you want?" "Yes," she whispered back.

We set up a time for her and her youth pastor to meet with an encourager from our staff. She dealt with many issues and lies in her belief system. During the next day of the conference, a young girl bounced up to me like Tigger from Winnie the Pooh. She was smiling ear to ear. She said, "I want to thank you for speaking this week and for the Steps to Freedom in Christ. I went through the whole thing and for the first time in my life, I feel free."

I was polite and said, "Thank you for your encouragement."

With a silly grin on her face, she smiled at me and said, "You don't know who I am, do you?"

"I'm afraid I don't," I replied. "Have we met before?"

"I was the girl you prayed for by the wall—remember?"

My jaw hit the floor. The girl standing before me was a totally different person—smiling, bubbly and animated. She had a peace and calm about her and hope for the future. How can such a change be explained? And can it last? Two year later I was speaking at Northwestern College chapel service in Minneapolis when the same young girl bounced up like Tigger to me to say "Hi." This time I recognized her. She was in her second year of Bible college and doing great.

Freedom can last. To show you how this works, we need to explain more about how our body (material, or outer, self), soul and spirit (immaterial, or inner, self) function in relationship with the external world and our Creator.

In the preceding chapter, we pointed out the connection between the brain and the mind. The brain records input from the external world through our five senses. It enables us to taste, smell, see, hear and feel. Every external input is recorded in the brain and processed by the mind. The mind is the compiler, interpreter and programmer in our computer analogy (the software). One cannot operate without the other.

HOW OUR COMPUTER GOT PROGRAMMED

Before we came to Christ, we were spiritually dead in our sins (see Eph. 2:1). In other words, we were born physically alive but spiritually dead. We did not experience the presence of God; we did not live or act like Him. We all learned to live our lives without God, as if we did not need Him. From our earliest days, our minds were programmed by the world around us. That is why the heart of an unsaved person is filled with lies and very sick (see Jer. 17:9).

Our view of life came from the environment around us: our home, the neighborhood we played in, the friends we had and the church we attended—or did not attend. We took in attitudes from bad experiences such as a death in the family, our parents' divorce and/or emotional, sexual or physical abuse. These lasting impressions, both good and bad, are burned into our minds over time.

We also live our lives according to what we choose to believe about ourselves and the world around us. We are not always aware that we continuously gather information that changes our beliefs. Many people cruise through life with a carefree attitude and are unaware of how the world in which they live influences them.

Our belief system is always changing as we process good and bad information and experiences. Unfortunately, not every piece of information we receive comes clearly marked as good or evil, true or false!

THE NECESSITY OF REPROGRAMMING OUR MINDS

Without Jesus, each of us would be nothing more than a product of our pasts. But Ezekiel prophesied that God would put a new heart and a new spirit within each of us (see Ezek. 36:26).

That actually happened when we accepted Christ as Savior. We became new creations (see 2 Cor. 5:17) and we now have the mind of Christ (see 1 Cor. 2:16) in the center of our beings (our inner selves).

Jesus was punished for our sins, so we might have new minds and walk free. We are even free from the punishment that everyone who sins deserves (see Rom. 8:1). Philip Yancey illustrates this point in his book *What's So Amazing About Grace*.

> In the movie *The Last Emperor*, the young child anointed as the last emperor of China lives in a magical life of luxury with a thousand eunuch servants at his command. "What happens when you do wrong?" his brother asks. "When I do wrong, someone else is punished," the boy emperor replies. To demonstrate, he breaks a jar, and one of the servants is beaten.
>
> In Christian theology, Jesus reversed that ancient pattern: when the servants erred, the King was punished. Grace is free only because the giver himself has borne the cost.[1]

If Jesus did that for us, then when we make mistakes, why don't we just change our thinking and feel better? Because everything that has been previously programmed into our computers from the world is still there, and it only takes a few seconds to recall it. Nobody pushed the clear button, because there is not one to push. Because the computer that is our mind has no delete button, it needs to be reprogrammed. The lies of this world must be replaced by the truth of God's Word. That is why Paul wrote, "And do not be conformed to this world, but be transformed by the renewing of your mind, that you may prove what the will of God is, that which is good and acceptable and perfect" (Rom. 12:2).

Before we came to Christ, each of us was conformed to this world—and we will continue to be as long as we allow it to influence us. In Christ, however, although our brains still receive and our minds still interpret messages from this world, we now have a new internal input, "which is Christ in you, the hope of glory" (Col. 1:27). The Spirit of truth will lead us into all truth, and that truth will set us free (see John 8:32).

At this point, you might be asking "If the truth sets us free, why do I still feel so bad?" In a general sense, we do not have direct control over feelings. We cannot *will* ourselves to feel good or like someone we hate. We can, however, exert indirect control of our emotions by what we *think* and *believe*.

Just as our glands are regulated by our central nervous system, so our emotions are primarily a product of our thoughts. The circumstances of life do not determine how we feel. Negative events do not cause depression. How we feel is primarily determined by *how we interpret life's events* (i.e., what we choose to think and believe) and secondarily by *how we choose to behave*. We can become depressed by failing to believe what God has said.

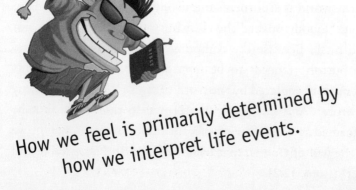

How we feel is primarily determined by how we interpret life events.

WHEN STRESS BECOMES DISTRESS

Let's look at the problem of stress. Some would say "But teen's don't experience stress!" Nothing is further from the truth. Today's teens experience a new level of stress. Walt Muller, the executive director of Parent/Youth Understanding, writes about "Sarah, an average teen."

Several years ago I asked teens to send me a list, ranking the five greatest pressures that they face. The results opened my eyes to the way things have changed.

One of the kids who responded was Sarah, a sixteen-year-old from New York. Her list was representative of the other lists I received. As number one she listed the pressure "looks." She was consumed with self-conscious worry about her hair, makeup, shape, and clothes. Next, she listed "grades for getting into the right college." Third was "drinking," with "sex" and "popularity" fourth and fifth.

Sarah's list was helpful, but the real eye-opener was what followed:

Walt, I suffer from a combination of anorexia and bulimia. It is very hard to recover from the devastations caused largely by pressure to be thin and to be perfect. I hope that I have helped.

I had never heard of anorexia and bulimia until I was twenty-one years old. Even then, I only knew one person who had had anorexia. Most of today's junior high girls know at least one friend who suffers from an eating disorder. Sarah not only had both but also knew about their causes and the difficult road to recovery.

Sarah and I began to correspond. She greatly helped me understand the pressures facing teens these days. Perhaps her story in her own words will give you the opportunity to peek into the window of the pressures, fears, and choices facing today's children and teens.

I come from an upper middle-class home. I'm a straight-A student, class president, and an over-achiever in every way. I don't really know why I am anorexic, but I think it's partly because I thought that if I got really sick, people would pay attention to me. The irony of it is that my father is a psychologist. He doesn't know.

My mother always compares her life to mine, so much that sometimes I feel smothered by her. I cannot talk to my father at all about important things. I never could. My father is home every evening at 6 P.M., but my mother is never home. She recently opened a business so she has to work from 9 A.M. until midnight. Sometimes she comes home to see me in afternoons, and sometimes she is around on weekends. Incidentally, my parents do not get along very well.

My mom says that if I get therapy, it will go on my record and may keep me out of Princeton or Amherst, the colleges to which I am applying.

I know my parents love me, but they think that I am so bright and capable that I don't need help or attention anymore. I just want people to realize that I don't have a perfect life and that I am lonely. I want people at school to notice me more and like me. Actually, I'm not at all sure what I want.

I have met many Sarahs over the years.[2]

What happens to us when we live under constant stress and pressure? When the pressures of life put demands on our physical system, our adrenal glands respond by secreting hormones into our physical bodies. This means that our bodies automatically respond to outside pressures—as in the natural "fight or flight" responses. If the pressures last too long, our adrenal glands cannot keep up, and stress becomes *dis*tress. The result can be physical illness or, in milder cases, we may become irritated about things that in less stressful times would not bother us physically or emotionally.

Why, then, do different people respond differently to the same stressful situation? Some actually seize the opportunity and thrive under the pressure, while others fall apart. What makes the difference? Does one have superior adrenal glands? We do not think so. Although we may differ considerably in our physical conditions, the major distinction lies in the software. It is not just the superior glands or outside factors such as deadlines, schedules, trauma and temptations that determine the degree of stress. The major variable is how we mentally view the world and process the information our brains receive.

Our minds can choose to respond by trusting God with the assurance of victory or by seeing ourselves as the helpless victims of circumstance. Do you remember the Israelites in the Old Testament? They viewed Goliath in reference to themselves, not in reference to God. To them, he was a huge giant. To God, Goliath was just a man with big feet. When the Israelites saw Goliath, they stressed out. David observed the same giant in reference to God and triumphed in the same situation that had left others in defeat. Faith in God (what we believe) greatly affects how we view and deal with the pressures of this world.

THE SPIRIT CAN AFFECT THE FLESH

Does the presence of Jesus the Wonderful Counselor transform the outer self or the inner self of a person? In other words, what physically changed in our lives at the moment we were born again? Nothing changed that was observable to the naked eye. In a similar fashion, we might ask what physical changes we observed on the outside of our computer when we loaded a new software program. Even though the same number of hardware components existed in the computer, the screen began to display a different image.

Would we begin to live differently if a new program were loaded into the computer that is our brain? There should be some change because our eyes have been opened to the truth, and the power of the Holy Spirit has enabled us to live by faith.

However, the change does not stop on the inside. The presence of God in our lives will slowly affect even our physical being. According to the words of Paul, "He who raised Christ Jesus from the dead will also give life to your mortal bodies through His Spirit who indwells you" (Rom. 8:11). This is

The presence of God in our lives will slowly affect even our physical being.

evident when we walk by the Spirit because "the fruit of the Spirit is love [the character of God], joy [the opposite of depression], peace [the opposite of anxiety], patience [the opposite of anger], kindness, goodness, faithfulness, gentleness, self-control" (Gal. 5:22-23). The connection between the initiating cause, which is the Spirit of truth working in our lives, and the end result, which is self-control, is the *mind*. The mind directs the brain, which in turn regulates all our glands and muscular movements.

BIBLICAL FAITH LEADS TO WHOLENESS

Jesus asked the blind men, "'Do you believe that I am able [to heal them]?' They said to Him, 'Yes, Lord.' Then He touched their eyes, saying, 'Be it done to you according to your faith'" (Matt. 9:28-29). The external power of Jesus was made effective by the blind men's choice to believe. In other words, the Lord chose to bring about a physical healing through the channel of their belief.

This is also true in every other way God works in our lives. We are saved by faith (see Eph. 2:8), sanctified by faith (see Gal. 3:3-5) and walk, or live, by faith (see 2 Cor. 5:7). God never bypasses the mind. He makes possible the renewing of our minds by His very presence. We respond in faith by choosing to believe the truth, to live by the power of the Holy Spirit and to not carry out the desires of the flesh (see Gal. 5:16).

Jesus is "the way [how we ought to live], and the truth [what we ought to believe], and the life [our spiritual union with God]" (John 14:6). Even the operation of spiritual gifts incorporates the use of our minds. Paul concludes, "I shall pray with the spirit and I shall pray with the mind also; I shall sing with the spirit and I shall sing with the mind also" (1 Cor. 14:15).

TRUTH AND THE BIOLOGICAL SYSTEM

Research strongly suggests a link between brain chemistry and hope. Our bodies are affected when we think we are helpless, hopeless and out of control. Symptoms of depression, such as sadness, despair, loss of appetite and sleep problems, increase. Once hope is restored, depression leaves.

This has major implications for people who struggle with depression and for those who minister to them. God established faith as the means by which we relate to Him and live our lives. Because He does not bypass our minds, then neither should we as we try to help others live whole and productive lives. If the way we perceive reality and choose to believe has an effect on our bodies and biochemistry, then treatment for depression should not be limited to medication.

WHAT ABOUT MEDICATION?

If God works through our faith, should we, as Christians, ever take medications for an emotional problem? Let's use an analogy to help sort out an answer. Consider a person who suffers regularly from acid indigestion because of his eating habits. Should he take medication to relieve the heartburn? Most people would, and there is nothing wrong with getting temporary relief. However, the long-term answer to this person's physical discomfort is to change his eating habits. We are what we eat, drink and breathe. Acid indigestion is our bodies' way of screaming, "Stop feeding me this junk!" Of course, in some cases there is also the possibility of a serious stomach illness such as an ulcer, cancer or a heart problem.

Taking medication to relieve pain is advisable, but the wise person will seek to discover the cause of the condition. In the vast majority of cases, a change in lifestyle will be necessary in order to regain good health. Good health is a product of a balanced routine of rest, exercise and diet.

No matter how well we learn to take care of our physical bodies, they are still destined to deteriorate over the course of our natural lives. Is this an argument to let our bodies go, never exercise and binge on junk food? Not at all! Our bodies are designed as temples of the Holy Spirit and meant to glorify God (see 1 Cor. 6:19-20).

Even with this God-given purpose, our hope does not lie in the preservation of our mortal bodies. Our hope lies in proven character (see Rom. 5:4) and the final resurrection when we will receive resurrected, immortal bodies. "Therefore we do not lose heart, but though our outer man is decaying, yet our inner man is being renewed day by day" (2 Cor. 4:16).

If negative thinking has affected a depressed person's neurochemistry, then taking antidepressants may be advisable to alleviate the depressed mood; but it is not the long-term solution in the vast majority of cases. The danger lies in establishing a person's hope in medication for the cure of depression instead of establishing hope in God and learning to live a balanced life according to His truth. However, we must also be open to the possibility that there really could be an organic brain problem or some other viral infection or chemical imbalance.

It is also possible that some of us will have to live with physical consequences of having been depressed over long periods of time. Lasting damage to the neurological system may make it necessary for a person to take medication, even for the rest of his life. That would be similar to the alcoholic who has done irreparable damage to his liver. The Lord may heal such a person in response to prayer, but Scripture gives no absolute assurance of that happening. There would be little incentive for us not to sin or believe incorrectly if all consequences were always miraculously removed.

In the Western world, we have been programmed by our culture to first search for every natural explanation; then if none is found, we conclude there is nothing left to do but pray. Yet the Bible does not quite put it like that. In the context of explaining how faith in God is the answer for anxiety, Jesus concluded, "But seek *first* His kingdom and His righteousness; and all these things shall be added to you. Therefore do not be anxious for tomorrow; for tomorrow will care for itself" (Matt. 6:33-34, emphasis added). When we struggle with emotional problems, go to God first, as He instructed us to do!

RENEGADE THOUGHTS

Renegade thoughts produce wandering, defiant and independent patterns of thinking that oppose the nature, character and Word of God. To entertain such notions leads to confusion and despair.

Here are some examples of renegade thoughts (there will be more on this in chapter 7).

- *I'm no good.*
- *God doesn't love me.*
- *I'm going to fail!*
- *I'm a failure.*
- *I'm going to lose* (or *going down*).
- *I'm stupid* (or *ugly* or *unlovable* or *arrogant*).

If the negative messages we receive from other people and we create ourselves are not enough, add to them the devil's attacks. He relentlessly accuses believers of all sorts of wrongdoings and weaknesses (see Rev. 12:10). Remember, the devil is a liar. Just because he says something does not make it true. In fact, most of his charges are false.

Finding the Truth

If what people believe does not conform to truth, then what they feel does not conform to reality.

We are continually making evaluations and judgments based on past experiences that affect our actions and our feelings. We think, *The mail carrier should have been here by now: I'll go and get the mail.* The thought about the mail carrier is a judgment call based on previous behavior and the reliability of the mail carrier.

When such a thought pops into your mind, you make a decision to go get the mail or wait until later. If you believe the mail carrier has not come, you are less likely to go check the mail. If you are anxiously waiting for an important piece of mail, you may get angry if the carrier shows up late. But the fact that the carrier was late does not make you angry. You become angry because you believe the carrier should have been there sooner, and the plans you made based on the carrier's timely arrival are dashed when he or she comes late. You would not have become angry if you had told yourself, *I have no right to expect the carrier to arrive at a time that is convenient for me, therefore I will patiently—patience is a fruit of the Spirit—wait until he or she comes.*

Take Every Thought Captive

The most damaging thoughts are lies about ourselves and God. That is the subject of the next two chapters, but we should note here that the apostle Paul makes a critical connection between thoughts we have toward God and the spiritual battle for our minds.

> For though we live in the world, we do not wage war as the world does. The weapons we fight with are not the weapons of the world. On the contrary, they have divine

power to demolish strongholds. We demolish arguments and every pretension that sets itself up against the knowledge of God, and we take captive every thought to make it obedient to Christ (2 Cor. 10:3-5, *NIV*).

Computer programmers have coined the term "GIGO," which means garbage in, garbage out. If we put garbage into our minds, we will probably live lives that look and smell a little bit like garbage. Jesus said, "The good man out of the good treasure of his heart brings forth what is good; and the evil man out of the evil treasure brings forth what is evil; for his mouth speaks from that which fills his heart" (Luke 6:45).

We have to be very careful what we put into our minds—hence the urgency of taking every thought captive and making it obedient to Christ. It does not make any difference whether the renegade thought originated from the television set, the Internet, a book, a speaker, our own memory bank or deceiving spirits. Even if it is a thought of our own, we must take *every* thought captive to the obedience of Christ.

If what we think is not true according to God's Word, then we should not pay attention to it. Instead, we should do what the apostle Paul says we should do:

Finally, brethren, whatever is true, whatever is honorable, whatever is right, whatever is pure, whatever is lovely, whatever is of good repute, if there is any excellence and if anything worthy of praise, let your mind dwell on these things (Phil. 4:8).

We do not get rid of negative thoughts by trying not to think them. Rather, we overcome them by choosing the truth and continuing to choose it until the negative thoughts are drowned out, or replaced, by the truth. If we want to experience the freedom

We do not get rid of negative thoughts by trying not to think them. Rather, we overcome them by choosing the truth.

that Christ purchased for us and the peace of mind that surpasses all understanding, then we must choose to think only those thoughts that are in perfect alignment with the Word of God.

DETECTING VIRUSES

Computer owners have been warned about the danger of viruses. A virus can cause severe damage to a program already loaded into the computer or to the hardware itself. Computer viruses are often not accidental but intentional. They may come from store-wrapped software that gets contaminated by disgruntled employees. Or the source may be some devious people who have purposefully created programs that are designed to introduce a harmful virus into any system that accesses them over the Internet or through sharing disks. Therefore, most computer systems have programs that scan for viruses. Similarly, we need to have the capability to stand against the deceiver, the devil.

It is not always easy to detect a virus in our own belief system, because the major strategy of the enemy is deception. Every

Christian is subject to tempting, accusing and deceiving thoughts. That is why we are to put on the armor of God. That is why we are to stand against the fiery darts Satan aims at our minds by taking up the shield of faith.

The most devious of Satan's schemes is deception. If you were tempted or accused, you would know it. But when you are deceived, you do not realize it is happening. That is why Jesus prays for those who follow Him, "I do not ask Thee to take them out of the world, but to keep them from the evil one. . . . Sanctify them in the truth; Thy word is truth" (John 17:15,17).

From the beginning, Eve was deceived and she believed a lie. Therefore, Paul writes, "But I am afraid, lest as the serpent deceived Eve by his craftiness, your minds should be led astray from the simplicity and purity of devotion to Christ" (2 Cor. 11:3). Commenting about the latter days of the Church Age, Paul also wrote, "But the Spirit explicitly says that in later times some will fall away from the faith, paying attention to deceitful spirits and doctrines of demons" (1 Tim. 4:1).

We have seen evidence of this around the world—people struggle with their thoughts, have difficulty concentrating and even hear strange voices. These voices or negative thoughts are usually self-condemning, suicidal, delusional and phobic. They result in feelings of guilt, hopelessness, sadness and deep despair.

How can our neurotransmitters fire in such a way that they produce thoughts that we oppose? It should not be difficult for a Christian to believe and understand that negative thoughts are the ongoing result of patterns of the flesh learned from living in a fallen world or the fiery darts from Satan that Scripture clearly warns us about. Unfortunately, a therapist with a secular worldview would never consider such possibilities.

In our experience, these symptoms usually indicate there is a battle for the person's mind. Instead of medication, or in addition to medication if the person is under a physician's care, we help such a person resolve personal and spiritual conflicts by encouraging him or her to submit to God and resist the devil (see Jas. 4:7). The intervention we use is outlined in the Steps to Freedom in Christ.

The apostle Paul spoke of "the peace of God, which surpasses all comprehension, [that] shall guard your hearts and your minds in Christ Jesus" (Phil. 4:7). Potentially, every born-again Christian should be able to experience this peace.

Sadly, most Christians do not experience this freedom in Christ; however, we believe that they can—God desires freedom for all of His children.

REPLACING LIES WITH LAUGHTER

We cannot experience the fruit of the Spirit if we believe a lie, dabble in the occult, hold on to bitterness, sink in pride, live in rebellion or sin without repentance. Depression is riddled with contaminated thinking and wrong beliefs built upon lies. "The LORD detests lying lips, but he delights in men who are truthful" (Prov. 12:22, *NIV*).

To illustrate this, let us close with the following testimony from a friend of our ministry:

A year ago, Simon fell captive to severe depression. The doctors did what they could, but without much effect. From time to time I had the opportunity to speak with him about the love of Christ, but he wasn't very responsive. Last fall we began to meet more frequently, but I always came away frustrated. Nothing seemed to change, and our conversations ran in circles around the same morbid themes. However, God used these times to show me that I was relying too much on my own efforts and not nearly enough on His power to effect change. In desperation, I was driven to seek God in a more profound way through prayer. God worked on Simon's distorted view of truth, while He worked to cut through the pride that was in my own heart. Just before Christmas, Simon made a commitment to follow Christ as Lord and Savior. His depression, however, was only mildly improved.

Simon had a history of occult and New Age involvement, and it became evident that there was demonic oppression in his life. For this reason, I lent him *The Bondage Breaker*.[3] At the end of the book, the believer is invited to walk through the seven "Steps to Freedom in Christ." I told Simon that I would help him work through these steps when I returned from a trip. During our time away, I called Simon to see how he was doing. The voice that spoke to me was changed. Simon had not waited for me to take him through the seven steps. He had done it himself the previous evening. The old thoughts which had constantly filled his mind were gone. I heard him laughing for the first time. Praise the Lord.

DEPRESSION BUSTERS

Read:

2 Corinthians 10:3-5

Reflect:

1. From our earliest days, our minds were programmed by what powerful forces (see Jer. 17:9)?
2. If the truth sets us free, then why are there times when we still feel bad and experience depression?
3. We know that at times depression has a physical cause. But list some of the possible spiritual causes of depression.
4. Why is taking every thought captive and destroying renegade thoughts that come into our minds so important when it comes to overcoming depression?
5. Why is deception one of Satan's most powerful devious schemes? And how does it relate to depression?

Respond:

Oh, Lord, I know that one of Satan's most powerful schemes is deception. It's my desire to learn how to take every thought captive to the obedience of Christ and destroy any renegade thoughts in my mind. Lord, I confess that at times I have believed that I was helpless. I renounce that lie and declare that I have all that I need for life and godliness. Lord, no matter how big or small, I want every lie to be exposed and replaced with the truth from Your Word. I know that what I believe can

even affect my body, so I ask You to show me Your truth so that
my body and my soul might begin to be healed. In Jesus' name
I pray. Amen.

Notes

1. Philip Yancey, *What's So Amazing About Grace* (Grand Rapids, MI: Zondervan Publishing House, 1997), n.p.
2. Walt Mueller, *Understanding Today's Youth Culture* (Wheaton, IL: Tyndale House Publishers, Inc., 1994), pp. 37-38.
3. Neil Anderson, *The Bondage Breaker* (Eugene, OR: Harvest House, 2000).

CHAPTER 5

SECRETS REVEALED—
UNDERSTANDING YOUR
HEAVENLY FATHER

*Now faith is the assurance of things hoped for, the conviction of
things not seen. And without faith it is impossible to please Him,
for he who comes to God must believe that He is, and that
He is a rewarder of those who seek Him.*

HEBREWS 11:1,6

*A five year old child's version of John 3:16: "For God so love the
world that he gave His only begotten Son, that whosoever believeth
in Him should not perish, but have ever laughing life."*

AUTHORS CARL AND ROSE SAMRA

In this chapter we look closely at faith and knowing our heavenly Father. Often as we go through life and experience its pains, we forget about God's unseen acts of love and mercy. We tend to see only the present problems of life and the accompanying pain. When we focus on the pain, we lose faith. This next story illustrates how easily we miss God's love and protection.

"Life's a little thing!" Robert Browning once wrote. But a little thing can mean a life. Even two lives. How well I remember. Two years ago in downtown Denver my friend Scott Reasoner and I saw a tiny and insignificant event change the world, but no one else seemed to notice.

It was one of those beautiful Denver days. Crystal clear and no humidity, not at cloud in the sky. We decided to walk the ten blocks to an outdoor restaurant rather than take the shuttle bus that runs up and down the Sixteenth Street Mall. The restaurant, in the shape of a baseball diamond, was called The Blake Street Baseball Club. Tables were set appropriately on the grass infield. Many colorful pennants and flags hung limply overhead.

As we sat outside, the sun continued to beat down on us, and it became increasingly hot. There wasn't a hint of a breeze, and the heat radiated up from the tabletop. Nothing moved, except the waiters, of course. And they didn't move very fast.

After lunch Scott and I started to walk back up the mall. We both noticed a young mother and her daughter who was holding her by the hand while reading a greeting card. It was immediately apparent to us that she was so engrossed in the card that she didn't notice a shuttle bus moving toward her at a good clip. She and her daughter were one step away from disaster when Scott started to yell. He hadn't even gotten a word out when a breeze blew the card out of her hand and over her shoulder. She spun around and grabbed the card nearly knocking over her daughter. By the time she picked up the card form the ground and turned back to cross the street, the shuttle bus had whizzed by her. She never knew what almost happened.

To this day, two things continue to perplex me about this event. Where did that one spurt of wind come from to blow the card out of that young mother's hand? There had not been a whisper of wind at lunch, or during our long walk up to the mall. Secondly, if Scott had been able to get his words out, the young mother might have looked up at us as they continued to walk into the bus. It was the wind that made her turn back to the card in the direction that saved her life and that of her daughter. The passing bus did not create the wind. On the contrary, the wind came from the opposite direction.

I have no doubt it was a breath from God protecting them both. But the awesomeness of this miracle is that she never knew. As we continued back to work, I wondered at how God often acts in our lives without our being aware. The difference between life and death can very well be a little thing.

Miracles often blow unseen through our lives![1]

God is at work in our lives everyday, what we now call 24/7. His unseen protection and love continue whether we realize they are at work or not. Because God is faithful, He never stops loving us.

AWAKENING FAITH

An attractive, talented 18-year-old woman made an appointment with me (Neil) to deal with a multitude of problems. She was the daughter of a pastor and had grown up in the Church. She had made a decision for Christ and was committed to follow Him.

Her immediate problem was a serious eating disorder. Reluctantly, she revealed a tormented secret life, which was riddled with starvation, manipulation, depression and thoughts of suicide. She was obsessed with her appearance and hated herself. Realizing this, I shared with her how Christ saw her. I reminded her that she was a loved, chosen daughter of the King. I told her she was a new creation in Christ and a personal friend of Jesus. Tears streaming down her face, she got to the core of her problem: "I wish I could believe that!"

Believing is not a matter of wishing. It is a matter of knowing and choosing. It is not something we feel like doing; it is

The only difference between non-Christian faith and Christian faith is the object of that faith.

something we choose to do based on what we have come to believe is true.

Faith is the operating principle of life. Everyone lives by faith. We drive our cars by faith, believing that they will run, that the road will be safe, that the traffic signs will be right, that the lights at the intersection will perform up to standard and that other people will drive safely. If we did not believe all of this, we would probably never get into a car or would at least be very anxious about driving.

We eat by faith, believing that canned food and packaged meat are safe. By eating the product, we show great faith in the rancher or farmer and the food processor. Our confidence is bolstered by the law, which is enforced by the Food and Drug Administration and by county health departments.

THREE PRINCIPLES OF FAITH

Faith is first and foremost dependent upon its object. The primary issue is not how much we believe, rather it is *what* or *whom* we believe in. The only difference between non-Christian faith and Christian faith is the object of that faith. Christian faith is not wishful thinking; it is based on truth revealed by God. The person and nature of God and His Word are the only valid objects of our faith. By contrast, non-Christians place faith in themselves, false gods, science, wealth, fame, other people and any of numerous other worldly objects, all of which fall short and some of which are outright deceptive.

The writer of the book of Hebrews lists in chapter 11 several biblical heroes who believed God. They had great faith because they believed in a great God. Then the writer says, "Remember those who led you, who spoke the word of God to you; and considering the result of their conduct, *imitate their faith*" (Heb. 13:7, emphasis added). He did not say that we should imitate what these heroes *did* but that we should imitate their faith—because what they believed is what determined their conduct. The next verse reveals the object of their faith: "Jesus Christ is the same yesterday and today, yes and forever" (v. 8).

The fact that God is immutable—which means He cannot change—makes Him the only reliable object for our faith. Nor can His Word change: "The grass withers, the flower fades, but the word of our God stands forever" (Isa. 40:8). The fact that God and His Word never change is what gives us stability in an ever-changing world. God is always faithful, and His Word is always true. Because God is faithful, we can live with the confidence that His promises are also true: "For as many as may be the promises of God, in Him they are yes" (2 Cor. 1:20).

Herein lies the basis for our hope, according to Hebrews 6:16-19:

> For men swear by one greater than themselves, and with them an oath given as confirmation is an end of every dispute. In the same way God, desiring even more to show to the heirs of the promise the unchangeableness of His purpose, interposed with an oath, in order that by two unchangeable things, in which it is impossible for God to lie, we may have strong encouragement, we who have fled for refuge in laying hold of the hope set before us. This hope we have as an anchor of the soul, a hope both sure and steadfast.

How Faith Grows

The second principle of faith is that it cannot be inauthentically pumped up. How much faith we have depends on how well we know the object of our faith. If we know seven promises from the

Word of God, the best we can have is a seven-promise faith. If we know 7,000 promises from God's Word, we can potentially have a 7,000-promise faith. That is why "faith comes from hearing, and hearing by the word of Christ" (Rom. 10:17).

Any attempt to step out on faith beyond that which we know to be true is presumption, not faith. If your faith is weak, then seek proper counsel to make sure that what you believe is indeed true. The consequences of trying to figure it out on your own are predictable: "Through presumption comes nothing but strife, but with those who receive counsel is wisdom" (Prov. 13:10). Remember, faith is dependent upon its object, and we are called by God to walk by faith according to what He says is true.

If I wanted to take away your hope, all I would have to do is distort your concept of God and of who you are as His child. Ask Christians who have been depressed for any length of time about their concept of God and what they believe about themselves. They question God or their salvation, and they believe things about themselves and God that are not true. Visit a psychiatric ward in a hospital and you will find some of the most religious people in the world. But what they believe about themselves and God is usually totally distorted.

To illustrate this second principle of faith, look at Psalm 13:

How long, O LORD? Will you forget me forever? How long will you hide your face from me? How long must I wrestle with my thoughts and every day have sorrow in my heart? How long will my enemy triumph over me? Look on me and answer, O LORD my God. Give light to my eyes, or I will sleep in death; my enemy will say, "I have overcome him," and my foes will rejoice when I fall. But I trust in your unfailing love; my heart rejoices in your salvation. I will sing to the LORD, for he has been good to me (vv. 1-6, NIV).

This psalm portrays King David with many of the classic symptoms of depression, including hopelessness, negative self-talk, thoughts of death and sadness. Even though he believes in God, David is depressed because what he believes about God is not true. How can an omnipresent and omniscient God forget David for even one minute, much less forever?

"Wrestling with my thoughts" is nothing more than talking to himself, which is not the answer. So David asks God to enlighten his eyes, and by the end of the psalm his reason has returned. He remembers that he has trusted in God's unfailing love and then expresses hope that his heart shall again rejoice. Finally, he exercises his will by singing to the Lord.

In this world where it is easy to lose perspective, how do you see life? As if there is no God or as if God is ever present?

> A young man was desperately seeking God. He sought out a wise old man who lived in a nearby beach house and posed the question: "Old man, how can I see God?" The old man who obviously knew God at a depth few of us experience, pondered the question for a very long time. At last he responded quietly: "Young man, I am not sure that I can help you—for you see, I have a very different problem. I cannot *not* see Him."[2]

Faith Determines Our Walk

If we really believe the truth, it will affect our walk and our talk. This is the third principle of faith.

If there were five frogs on a log and three decided to jump off, how many would be left on the log? The answer is five—we only said that three *decided* to jump off. They may have come to this decision because they thought it was the right thing to do, but it is only wishful thinking until they actually hop off the log.

"But someone may well say, 'You have faith, and I have works; show me your faith without the works, and I will show you my faith by my works'" (Jas. 2:18). James is not contradicting the truth that we are saved by faith and by faith alone. He is saying that the way we live our lives reveals what we believe. People will not always live according to what they profess, but they will always live according to what they believe. The road to hell is paved with good intentions, and the apparent profession of faith by some is just wishful thinking.

The same can be said about hope. When somebody says "Oh, I hope so," that person probably means "Wouldn't it be nice if that were really true!" That is not biblical hope. Hope is the present *assurance* of some future good based on the Word of God.

> Now faith is the assurance of things hoped for, the conviction of things not seen. And without faith it is impossible to please Him, for he who comes to God must believe that He is, and that He is a rewarder of those who seek Him (Heb. 11:1,6).

If you want to experience the blessings of God, hop off the log! "If you know these things, you are blessed if you do them" (John 13:17).

In the Bible, the English words "faith," "trust" and "belief" all derive from the same original Greek word. Believing something is not just giving mental assent to something. Scriptural belief is a demonstrated reliance in the object of faith.

It is also important to understand that believing something does not make it true. In Christianity, the Word of God is true; therefore, we believe it and we will live accordingly by faith. Believing does not make it true, and not believing does not make it false. Truth is truth whether we believe it or not. According to Paul, if we renew our minds according to the truth of God's

Truth is truth whether we believe it or not.

Word, we prove that the will of God is good, acceptable and perfect (see Rom. 12:2), and other people will see this truth as they observe how we live our lives.

New Age philosophy distorts this. In New Age thought, if you believe hard enough, it will become true. That is false. New Age teachers would also have us believe that we can create reality with our minds. To do that we would have to be God, and that is exactly what they claim to be. That is the same lie the devil tried to get Eve to believe in the Garden of Eden. We are created in God's image, but we are not God. We do not create reality with our minds; we respond to reality by faith according to what God says is true. God has not given us the right to determine what is true or false. He has given us the privilege of responding by faith to what He has said is true.

Suppose you just bought a new computer, but you did not bother to look at the manufacturer's handbook that explains how it should work. You attempt to use it the way you think it should work, but it will not start. That computer was designed to operate only one way. Any attempt to use it any other way will fail.

Similarly, the wise man said, "There is a way which seems right to a man, but its end is the way of death" (Prov. 14:12). God created us in His image and told us what the truth is and how we are to live by faith. Jesus said, "I am the way, and the truth, and the life" (John 14:6). Try another way and we will be lost. Believe something other than the truth as revealed by God and we will never become the people God created us to be, nor experience the freedom of forgiveness He purchased for us on the cross. If we try to "get a life" other than the life of Christ, we will remain dead in our trespasses and sins.

DISTORTION AND DAMAGE

The nature of God will never change, but our perception of Him has been changed if it has been filtered through the grid of living in a fallen world.

Note the following diagram. We have seen good students of the Bible point to the left side of the diagram when asked which side reveals the true nature of God. But when asked how they feel about God in their personal experience, they pointed to the right side! Somehow during their experience of growing up, they entertained thoughts about God that were not true.

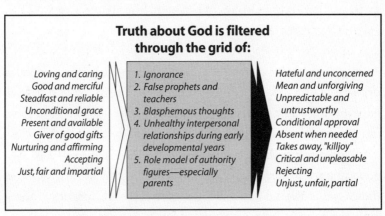

Truth about God is filtered through the grid of:

Loving and caring	1. Ignorance	*Hateful and unconcerned*
Good and merciful	2. False prophets and teachers	*Mean and unforgiving*
Steadfast and reliable	3. Blasphemous thoughts	*Unpredictable and untrustworthy*
Unconditional grace	4. Unhealthy interpersonal relationships during early developmental years	*Conditional approval*
Present and available		*Absent when needed*
Giver of good gifts		*Takes away, "killjoy"*
Nurturing and affirming	5. Role model of authority figures—especially parents	*Critical and unpleasant*
Accepting		*Rejecting*
Just, fair and impartial		*Unjust, unfair, partial*

Remember: *If what we believe does not conform to truth, then what we feel does not conform to reality.* Consequently, there are young people sitting in youth groups all over the world who intellectually know that God loves them but do not feel loved or saved. It would be safe to say that each of us has come up with some thoughts against the knowledge of God. But we have divinely powerful spiritual weapons to tear down those strongholds (see 2 Cor. 10:3-5).

LOVING AND KNOWING GOD

Matthew records the time an unnamed Pharisee asked Jesus the question, "Teacher, which is the great commandment in the Law?" (Matt. 22:36). Today we are more inclined to ask, "God, what is the secret for living a successful and victorious life?" For either question, Christ's answer is the same:

> "You shall love the Lord your God with all your heart, and with all your soul, and with all your mind." This is the great and foremost commandment. The second is like it, "You shall love your neighbor as yourself." On these two commandments depend the whole Law and the Prophets (Matt. 22:37-40).

The whole purpose for having the Bible is to govern our relationship with God and humankind. We are commanded to love God more for our sake than for His. He does not need our love, but we need to love Him.

The commandment to love God is not a directive to feel good about Him. How we feel is the product of what we choose to believe. However, a joyful countenance would certainly follow if we really knew Him, because to know God is to love Him.

- We need to know that God is love and that He is beautiful beyond comprehension.

- We need to know that God is omnipresent (everywhere). No matter where we go, God is there.
- We need to know that He is omniscient (all knowing). He knows the thoughts and intentions of our hearts.
- We need to know that God is omnipotent (all powerful). Consequently, we can do all things through Christ who strengthens us (see Phil. 4:13).

God is faithful and true. God is light and in Him is no darkness at all. He is holy and just.

DEPRESSION BUSTERS

Read:

Hebrews 11:1-6

Reflect:

1. Why do we tend to focus on the present and visual problems of life and the pains of this world, rather than God? What can be damaged if we do?
2. Why is it so easy to miss God's displays of love and protection in our everyday lives? How can we focus more on Him?
3. What are the three principles of faith taught in this chapter?
4. How is true faith built up or increased in a believer's life?

5. Why should true faith have an effect on our life and Christian walk? How should it affect what we do and say?

Respond:

Dear Lord, You said that without faith it is impossible to please You, for he who comes to God must believe that You are a rewarder of those who seek You. Lord, I believe in You and know that You want what is best for me in my life. I confess that I have believed lies about You and not trusted the truth of Your Word. Forgive me for my lack of faith. I choose now to put my trust in You and to believe that You are loving and all powerful, kind and merciful, even when the circumstances of my life seem to tell me something different. I will trust You. In Jesus' name I pray. Amen.

Notes

1. Yitta Halverstam and Judith Leventhal, *Small Miracles II* (Avon, MA: Adams Media Corporation, 1999), n.p.
2. Alice Gray, comp., *Stories for the Extreme Teen's Heart* (Sisters, OR: Multnomah Publishers, 2000), p. 258.

CHAPTER 6

OVERCOMING BARRIERS TO KNOWING GOD—BREAKING DOWN THE WALL

But whatever things were gain to me, those things I have counted as loss for the sake of Christ. More than that, I count all things to be loss in view of the surpassing value of knowing Christ Jesus my Lord.

PHILIPPIANS 3:7-8

A Bible that is falling apart probably belongs to someone who isn't.

REV. CHRISTIAN JOHNSON

FROM DISTANCE TO INTIMACY

We can intellectually know all about our heavenly Father and not really know Him at all. In the same way, we can know all about Abraham Lincoln. He was the sixteenth president of the United States of America. He knew a lot of the Bible and quoted it frequently. John Wilkes Booth shot President Lincoln in April 1865. We know these and many more facts about Abraham Lincoln; but we have never met him, nor do we know him personally. Similarly, knowing about God and spending time with Him are very different things.

Jesus said, "Look I stand at the door and knock. If you hear me calling and open the door, I will come in, and we will share a meal as friends" (Rev. 3:20, *NLT*).

Paul knew all about God from an Old Testament perspective. He was taught by the best. He was a Hebrew of Hebrews, a Pharisee who kept the law and was found blameless until Christ struck him down on the Damascus road. Reflecting on his past self-righteousness, Paul wrote:

The Bible also declares that nothing can separate us from the love of God.

But whatever things were gain to me, those things I have counted as loss for the sake of Christ. More than that, I count all things to be loss in view of the surpassing value of knowing Christ Jesus my Lord, for whom I have suffered the loss of all things, and count them but rubbish in order that I may gain Christ (Phil. 3:7-8).

Paul no longer just knew *about* God. Now he *knew* Him. He realized that he was a child of the King and that he was in a love relationship with his heavenly Father.

From Rebellion to Obedience

If you have accepted Christ as your Savior, you have a relationship with God. But many Christians are not living very close to Him. Let us explain. When we were born physically, we each had a relationship with our earthly father. Could we do anything that would change the fact that we were related to him? What if we ran away? Would we still be related? What if our father kicked us out of the house? Nothing would change the fact that we are related by blood. It is a biological fact.

But could we do some things that would cause us to no longer live at peace with our earthly fathers? Sure—and we probably discovered almost every way by the time we were five years old. Although living in harmony with our fathers has nothing to do with our blood relationship, it has everything to do with trusting and obeying.

This was even true of Jesus: "Although He was a Son, He learned obedience from the things which He suffered" (Heb. 5:8). We also learned to trust and obey our earthly fathers. If we did not, chances are the relationship we had with them was not very personal and we really did not know them other than as taskmasters or absentee parents.

Now that we are children of God, is there anything we can do that would change the fact that we are related to our heavenly Father? The answer is the same, and for the same reason. We are blood related.

You were not redeemed with perishable things like silver or gold from your futile way of life inherited from your forefathers, but with precious blood, as of a lamb unblemished and spotless, the blood of Christ. For you have been born again not of seed which is perishable but imperishable, that is, through the living and abiding word of God (1 Pet. 1:18-19,23).

The Bible also declares that nothing can separate us from the love of God (see Rom. 8:35), and no one can snatch us out of the Father's hand (see John 10:28). Our eternal life is not dependent on our ability to hold on to Him in our strength; it is primarily dependent upon His ability to hold on to us. The Lord said, "I will never desert you, nor will I ever forsake you" (Heb. 13:5). Not only that, but he has also declared, "You were sealed in Him with the Holy Spirit of promise, who is given as a pledge of our inheritance" (Eph. 1:13-14).

FROM DEFEAT TO VICTORY

We can be related to our heavenly Father as His children, but our relationship with Him will not be very personal or intimate and our knowledge of Him will be very shallow if we do not learn to trust and obey Him. Although our destiny may not be at stake, our daily victory is.

If two people are going to grow closer to each other, they must overcome any problems that happen between them. You may desire to know a new kid at school better, but you will not be

If two people are going to grow closer to each other, they must overcome any problems that happen between them. The same holds true in our relationship with God.

able to befriend him if you have offended him or if he has offended you. First, you would have to forgive and seek forgiveness.

The same holds true in our relationship with God. You will not be able to relate personally to God and get to know Him better until you get right with Him. Even your ability to read the Bible and understand truth will be hampered until you have resolved personal and spiritual conflicts that affect your relationship with God.

You must also straighten things out with other people. Remember, the great commandments are to love the Lord your God with your total being, and your neighbor as yourself.

Paul teaches that these problems must be resolved before we can understand God's Word:

I gave you milk to drink, not solid food; for you were not yet able to receive it. Indeed, even now you are not yet able, for you are still fleshly. For since there is jealousy and strife among you, are you not fleshly, and are you not walking like mere men? (1 Cor. 3:2-3, emphasis added).

We have observed this happening around the world. Young Christians try to read their Bibles, but it does not make any sense to them. They try to pray, but it is like talking to the wall. They hear a message at youth group, but it goes in one ear and out the other. It is not enough to know the Word of God; we each need the life of Christ present within us if we are to change. We have had the privilege of encouraging thousands of teenagers and helping them work through personal issues by taking them through the Steps to Freedom in Christ. After getting radically right with God, teens report that now they can read the Bible and understand what it says. Jesus becomes a personal friend, instead of a religious icon.

The discipleship counseling process and biblical principles that have helped other teens resolve their relationships with God can help you resolve the issues that are critical between yourself and God. Let's take a look at these issues.

Counterfeit Versus Real

When early Christians made a public confession of faith, they would stand, face the west and say, "I renounce you, Satan, and all your works and all your ways." This was the first step in repentance.

In addition to that broad statement, Christians would specifically renounce every one of their counterfeit religious experiences, every false vow or pledge they had made and every false teacher or doctrine they had believed. We encourage every person we counsel to do the same.

"Renounce" means "to give up a claim or a right." To renounce means that you make a definite decision to let go of past commitments, pledges, vows, pacts and beliefs that are not Christian. "He who conceals his sins does not prosper, but whoever confesses and renounces them finds mercy" (Prov. 28:13, *NIV*).

Some people commit themselves to Christ and choose to believe the Word of God, but they hold on to past commitments and beliefs. That would make salvation a process of addition, instead of a transformation.

Every believer must decisively let go of the past, which is the first step in genuine repentance. If we totally embrace the truth, then we also define what is not true. The apostle Paul reveals the close link between renouncing the past and not losing heart for the future (not being depressed or discouraged):

> Therefore, since we have this ministry, as we received mercy, we do not lose heart, but we have renounced the things hidden because of shame, not walking in craftiness or adulterating the word of God, but by the manifestation of truth commending ourselves to every man's conscience in the sight of God (2 Cor. 4:1-2).

Paul is contrasting the truth of divine revelation with that of false teachers and prophets. Knowing God's holiness and His call for Church purity, Paul asks us to renounce every immoral practice, every distortion of truth and any deceitfulness of the heart.

God does not take lightly false guidance and false teachers. In Old Testament times such teachers were to be stoned to death, and there were serious consequences for those who consulted them. "As for the person who turns to mediums and to spiritists, to play the harlot after them, I will also set My face against that person and will cut him off from among his people" (Lev. 20:6). Similar warnings about false teachers and false prophets are found in the New Testament. That is why it is necessary to renounce any and all involvement with false guidance, false teachers, false prophets and every cult and occult practice. We do not want to be cut off by God; we want to be connected to Him.

DECEPTION VERSUS TRUTH

The ultimate battle is between the Kingdom of light and the kingdom of darkness, between Christ and the antichrist, between good and evil, between the Spirit of truth and the father of lies. Therefore, an important step in being set free from depression is the process of sorting out the lies from the truth, and then choosing what is right.

We are told to speak the truth in love (see Eph. 4:15,25) and to walk in the light (see 1 John 1:7). Many people who struggle with depression believe lies, walk in darkness and avoid intimate contact with others. In order to overcome depression and live free in Christ, we must choose the truth by winning the battle for our minds. This requires an uncompromising commitment to God's Word.

The first step in recovery is to admit that we have a problem and then find at least one person with whom we can be totally honest. The worst thing we can do is to isolate ourselves and sit alone with our troubled thoughts.

An anxious person is double minded, and James writes that a double-minded person is unstable in all his ways (see Jas. 1:8). Jesus said, "No one can serve two masters; for either he will hate the one and love the other, or he will hold to one and despise the other. . . . For this reason I say to you, do not be anxious for your life" (Matt. 6:24-25). We cannot have mental peace or emotional health if we are double minded.

BITTERNESS VERSUS FORGIVENESS

We have never met a depressed teen who is not struggling with bitterness. Depressed people carry the emotional scars and bear the pain of wounds others have inflicted upon them. They have never known how to let go of the past and forgive from the heart. Some have chosen not to get better. They hang on to their anger because they think it will protect them from being hurt again—but they are only hurting themselves even more.

Forgiveness is the key to overcoming bitterness. Through forgiveness the captive is set free—and once the captive is set free, only then do we discover that we were the captive! We cannot be liberated from our past or be emotionally free in the present without forgiving from the heart. The future threat of torture that Christ promised to the unforgiving (see Matt. 18:34) turns out to be a present reality.

But God is not out to get us; He is out to restore us. He knows that if we hang on to our bitterness, we will only hurt ourselves and others (see Heb. 12:15). As Paul said, "Let all bitterness and wrath and anger and clamor and slander be put away from you, along with all malice. And be kind to one another, tender-hearted, forgiving each other, just as God in Christ also has forgiven you" (Eph. 4:31-32).

We forgive others for our own sakes and for the sake of our relationship with God. What is to be gained in forgiving others

God is not out to get us; He is out to restore us.

is freedom. We are also warned by Paul that we need to forgive others so that Satan does not take advantage of us (see 2 Cor. 2:10-11). This critical issue must be resolved if we are to find freedom from depression. Trying to overcome depression while holding on to our bitterness is like expecting physical well-being while simultaneously eating both healthy foods and poison.

REBELLION VERSUS SUBMISSION

We live in a rebellious age. Many people seem to think it is their right to criticize and sit in judgment of those who are in authority over them. Those with a rebellion problem may have the worst problem in the world. Scripture instructs us to submit to and pray for those who are in authority over us. Honoring our mother and father is the first of the Ten Commandments that is accompanied by a promise (see Eph. 6:1-2). The New Testament clearly calls for submission to authorities:

> Let every person be in subjection to the governing authorities. For there is no authority except from God, and those which exist are established by God. Therefore he who resists authority has opposed the ordinance of God; and they who have opposed will receive condemnation upon themselves. For rulers are not a cause of fear for good behavior, but for evil. Do you want to have no fear of authority? Do what is good, and you will have praise from the same (Rom. 13:1-3).

There may be times when we must obey God rather than humans (see Acts 5:29). When a human authority requires that we do something that is forbidden by God and restricts us from doing what God has called us to do, then we must obey God rather than a human. The same principle applies when someone tries to exercise control over us when it exceeds the scope of his authority. A policeman can write a ticket if we break a traffic law, but he cannot tell us what to believe or prevent us from going to church. It is proper to protect ourselves from abuse; however, we will rarely have to do that.

It takes a great act of faith to trust God to work through authority figures who are less than perfect, but that is what He asks us to do. This is critical for a right relationship with God, and such a relationship is essential for complete recovery from depression.

PRIDE VERSUS HUMILITY

Depressed young people are usually filled with shame and guilt, whether it is real or imagined. Pride often keeps them locked in a pattern of false thinking that robs them of the help they need. *I should be able to work this out myself!* they commonly think. That is tragic, because we were never intended to live this life alone. God created Adam and Eve to live dependent upon Him. All temptation is essentially an attempt to get us to live our lives independent of God.

Pride is an independent spirit that wants to exalt self. "God is opposed to the proud, but gives grace to the humble" (Jas. 4:6). Pride says, "I can do this. I can get out of this myself." Oh, no, we can't! Such arrogant thinking sets us up for a fall because "pride goes before destruction, and a haughty spirit before stumbling" (Prov. 16:18). We absolutely need God and we need each other. Paul says, "We . . . glory in Christ Jesus and *put no confidence in the flesh*" (Phil. 3:3, emphasis added).

Shame and self-deprecation are not humility. Humility is confidence properly placed. That is why we put no confidence in our flesh; our confidence is in God. Any attempt to be self-sufficient robs us of our true sufficiency in Christ because only in Christ can we do all things (see Phil. 4:13). God intended for His children to live victoriously by having great confidence in Christ and in His ability to make us able. "Not that we are adequate in ourselves to consider anything as coming from ourselves, but our adequacy is from God, who also made us adequate as servants of a new covenant, not of the letter, but of the Spirit; for the letter kills, but the Spirit gives life" (2 Cor. 3:5-6).

BONDAGE VERSUS FREEDOM

It has been estimated that 25 percent of those who struggle with severe depression are chemically addicted. This addiction may be to prescription drugs, alcohol or street drugs. Drowning sorrows in drugs and alcohol only adds to the downward spiral of depression.

On the other hand, the fear of becoming addicted to prescription drugs has kept many people from taking antidepressants, which might help them. That is unfortunate because the possibility of becoming addicted to antidepressants when properly administered is virtually nil.

There is also a strong correlation between depression and sexual bondage. Many girls who struggle with depression have been sexually abused, and many depressed young men are sex addicts. Addictive behavior is degrading and spiritually defeating for those who are supposed to be alive in Christ and dead to sin (see Rom. 6:11). The sin-and-confess cycle only adds to feelings of defeat and depression. If the bondage is not broken, the sin is likely to be repeated.

We believe that Christ is the only answer for anyone who is in bondage to sin, and that the truth of God's Word will set them free. If you are struggling with a sexual bondage, we encourage you to check out two of our books, *Purity Under Pressure* and *Ultimate Love*.

Habitual sin keeps a person in bondage, which is very depressing to those who want to live free in Christ. Paul wrote,

> The night is almost gone, and the day is at hand. Let us therefore lay aside the deeds of darkness and put on the armor of light. Let us behave properly as in the day, not in carousing and drunkenness, not in sexual promiscuity and sensuality, not in strife and jealousy. But put on the Lord Jesus Christ, and make no provision for the flesh in regard to its lusts (Rom. 13:12-14).

Repentance and faith in God are the only answers for breaking the bondage to the sin that so easily entangles us. We can be free from such bondage, because every believer is alive in Christ and dead to sin (see Rom. 6:11).

CURSES VERSUS BLESSINGS

The last step in helping teens find freedom in Christ is to renounce the sins of *the past*. The Ten Commandments reveal that the sins of our ancestors can be passed down to the third and fourth generation. This is evident in our society by the well-documented cycles of abuse. Jesus said:

> Woe to you, scribes and Pharisees, hypocrites! For you build the tombs of the prophets and adorn the monuments of the righteous, and say, "If we had been living in the days of our fathers, we would not have been partners with them in shedding the blood of the prophets."

Consequently you bear witness against yourselves, that
you are sons of those who murdered the prophets (Matt.
23:29-31).

In other words, "Like father, like son." We are not *guilty* of
our fathers' sins, but because they sinned, we will have to live
with the consequences of their sin. And we are doomed to continue to live in the way we were taught by them unless we repent.
"A pupil is not above his teacher; but everyone, after he has been
fully trained, will be like his teacher" (Luke 6:40). The primary
teachers in the first five years of our lives were our parents, and
much of our personality and temperament was established in
those early and formative years of our lives.

When God's Old Covenant believers repented, they con-
fessed their sins and the sins of their fathers (see Lev. 26:39-40;
Neh. 1:6; 9:2; Jer. 14:20; Dan. 9:10-11). We have the same responsibility today, "knowing that you were not redeemed with perishable things like silver or gold from your futile way of life *inherited from your forefathers*, but with precious blood, as of a lamb
unblemished and spotless, the blood of Christ" (1 Pet. 1:18-19,
emphasis added).

Every born-again Christian is a child of God and a new creation in Christ. Do not let incomplete repentance, a lack of faith
in Him and unresolved conflicts keep you from experiencing
your freedom in Christ. This lack of connectedness with God
often results in depression.

HELP IS AVAILABLE

In our curriculum *Busting Free,* we describe the discipleship
process that has helped thousands of people resolve their conflicts and find freedom in Christ. Ultimately, God is our only
hope, and we must live in harmony with Him if we are going to

be free from depression. These issues must be resolved and they can be. You can resolve these personal and spiritual conflicts on your own by going through the Steps to Freedom in Christ (found in Neil's book *Finding Hope Again*).

Those who are severely depressed will also need the help and objectivity of a trained encourager. Such was the case of a girl who attended one of my (Neil's) seminars in Europe. She shared the following testimony:

> I was born and raised in a very legalistic and abusive "Christian" home. Church attendance was mandatory, but the physical and emotional abuse I suffered at the hands of my parents distorted my concept of God. In our church was a large sign that said, "God is love." But I had no idea what love was. If what I experienced at home was supposed to be the love of God, then I wanted no part of it. I moved away from my parents to attend college and get away from God. I studied psychology and worked as a professional counselor. During this time I suffered continuously from depression. Finally I realized that I couldn't help myself, much less others, so I went into educational psychology and finally into vocational psychology.
>
> In desperation, I started to attend an international church. A Sunday School class was going through a video series by Neil Anderson. I learned who I was supposed to be in Christ and finally someone explained to me the battle that was going on in my mind. I found out that there were trained encouragers at the church who were taking people through the Steps to Freedom in Christ. I made an appointment with great apprehension and much fear. I didn't know what to expect but I knew I had nothing to lose and possibly much to gain.

It was an amazing encounter with God. I could feel the layers of self-righteousness, pride, rebellion and sin come off. Every step was meaningful to me, but the biggest release came when I forgave my parents for their abuse and for distorting my concept of God. As soon as I was done, I knew I was free from years of living in bondage to the lies I have believed about God and myself. And I was connected to God in a living and liberating way. His Spirit was now bearing witness with my spirit that I was a child of God. I was set free. I never struggled with depression again.

THE GOD OF ALL COMFORT

God is your protection.

You are my refuge and my shield; I have put my hope in your word (Ps. 119:114, *NIV*).

God is always available when you need help.

God is our refuge and strength, an ever-present help in trouble (Ps. 46:1, *NIV*).

God will not abandon you.

I will never leave you nor forsake you (Josh. 1:5, *NIV*).

God will comfort you in times of trouble.

Praise be to the God and Father of our Lord Jesus Christ, the Father of compassion and the God of all comfort, who comforts us in all our troubles, so that we can comfort those in any trouble with the comfort we ourselves have received from God (2 Cor. 1:3-4, *NIV*).

God has a plan for you.

"For I know the plans I have for you," declares the LORD, "plans to prosper you and not to harm you, plans to give you hope and a future. Then you will call upon me and come and pray to me, and I will listen to you. You will seek me and find me when you seek me with all your heart" (Jer. 29:11-13, *NIV*).

God knows you intimately.

For you created my inmost being; you knit me together in my mother's womb. I praise you because I am fearfully and wonderfully made; your works are wonderful, I know that full well (Ps. 139:13-14, *NIV*).

God longs to help those who are hurting.

The LORD is close to the brokenhearted and saves those who are crushed in spirit (Ps. 34:18, *NIV*).

DEPRESSION BUSTERS

Read:

2 Corinthians 4:1-2

Reflect:

1. How is it that we can intellectually know all about our heavenly Father and not really know Him at all?
2. Why do some people, even though they have accepted Christ as their Savior and have a relationship with Him, still not walk or live very close to Him?
3. List the Seven Steps to Freedom in Christ that are outlined in this chapter.
4. Of the Seven Steps to Freedom in Christ, which do you feel you need to hear from the Lord about?

Respond:

Dear Lord, You said, "Look! Here I stand at the door and knock. If you hear me calling and open the door, I will come in, and we will share a meal as friends" (Rev. 3:20, NLT). Lord, I know at times I have locked You out of my life and thus opened the door to depression and sin. I confess that I have allowed depression and sin to have their way in my life. I know that I can never be free from depression until I am right with You. So I ask You to reveal to me any doors that I have opened to depression and sin. I want to be free and walk close to You. Thank You for Your love and mercy. In Jesus' name I pray. Amen.

CHAPTER 7

HOUSE OF STONE—
UNDERSTANDING
YOURSELF

*We know that, when He appears, we shall be like Him, because we shall
see Him just as He is. And everyone who has this hope fixed on Him
purifies himself, just as He is pure.*

1 JOHN 3:2-3

Find joy in everything that leads to God.

TERESA OF AVILA

Depression is *primarily* a software (mental programming) problem rather than a hardware (brain) problem. The Christian psychiatrists with whom we have talked estimate that medication is probably essential only in 10 percent of all the cases diagnosed as depression.

If the problem is primarily due to the software, then how much of the problem is mental and how much is spiritual?

THE PRIMARY BATTLEFIELD: THE MIND

The answer is seldom either/or; rather, it is usually both/and. Spiritual problems are also mental problems because the spiritual battle is waged in the mind. To solve the problem of depression, we need a complete answer that takes into account all reality. The least understood and therefore most often neglected piece of the puzzle is the spiritual battle that is going on in the minds of young people around the world.

Scripture clearly warns us about the reality of the kingdom of darkness. Paul said, "I am afraid, lest as the serpent deceived Eve by his craftiness, your minds should be led astray from the simplicity and purity of devotion to Christ" (2 Cor. 11:3). He also wrote, "The Spirit explicitly says that in later times some will fall away from the faith, paying attention to deceitful spirits and doctrines [teachings] of demons" (1 Tim. 4:1).

We have counseled hundreds of teens who are struggling with their thoughts, who have difficulty concentrating or reading their Bible, and there are many others who actually hear voices in their heads. In the majority of cases, these common symptoms are evidence of a spiritual battle for their minds. This spiritual battle requires spiritual protection and weaponry. Again Paul writes:

Finally, be strong in the Lord, and in the strength of His might. Put on the full armor of God, that you may be able to stand firm against the schemes of the devil. For our struggle is not against flesh and blood, but against the rulers, against the powers, against the world forces of this darkness, against the spiritual forces of wickedness in the heavenly places. Therefore, take up the full armor of God, that you may be able to resist in the evil day, and having done everything, to stand firm. Stand firm therefore, having girded your loins with truth, and having put on the breastplate of righteousness, and having shod your feet with the preparation of the gospel of peace; in addition to all, taking up the shield of faith with which you will be able to extinguish all the flaming missiles of the evil one (Eph. 6:10-16).

THE PRIMARY PROTECTION

The "heavenly places" are a present reality. The *New International Version* of the Bible translates this phrase as "heavenly realms." This phrase does not refer to heaven where God has His throne, nor does it refer to some physical planet, such as Pluto or Mars, that exists in the natural realm. It refers to the spiritual world, or atmosphere, in which we live. The god (ruler) of this world, "your enemy the devil prowls around like a roaring lion looking for someone to devour" (1 Pet. 5:8, *NIV*).

John says, "We know that we are of God, and the whole world lies in the power of the evil one" (1 John 5:19). Herein lies the problem and the answer in one verse. People are kept in spiritual bondage because of the lies they believe about God and themselves, and Satan is the father of lies (see John 8:44).

Jesus is the truth (see John 14:17), and the Holy Spirit is the Spirit of truth. He will guide you into all truth (see John 16:13), and that truth will set you free (see John 8:32). That is possible because we are children of God.

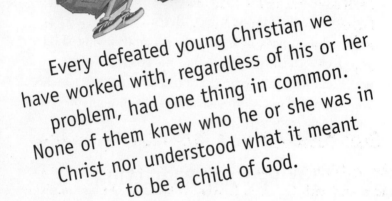

Every defeated young Christian we have worked with, regardless of his or her problem, had one thing in common. None of them knew who he or she was in Christ nor understood what it meant to be a child of God.

Every defeated young Christian we have worked with, regardless of his or her problem, had one thing in common. None of them knew who he or she was in Christ nor understood what it meant to be a child of God. Almost all of them questioned their salvation. If the Holy Spirit is bearing "witness with our spirit that we are children of God" (Rom. 8:16), then why were they not sensing it? "Because you are sons, God has sent forth the Spirit of His Son into our hearts, crying, 'Abba! [or] Father!'" (Gal. 4:6). Where is the "Abba! Father!" in the depth of depression? He is there, but depressed people often do not sense His presence because of ignorance or lack of genuine repentance. This true story by Janis Whipple shows the Father's love:

It was cold, gray January morning. I'd gone to the beach to walk. I had a lot on my mind, and I wanted to be alone. I wanted to feel close to God again. As I walked, I picked up a stick and wrote in the sand. I named four things that had hurt me and disappointed God. And I wrote the word peace, which I wanted, but did not have. I dropped the stick and kept going. As I walked, I prayed, crying on God's shoulder.

When I noticed the tide coming in, I turned back. I looked for the words I had written. The stick was there, but the water had washed away all the words except one: peace. God had washed away my pain and left a promise of peace.[1]

OUR IDENTITY AND POSITION IN CHRIST

The devil does not want us to know that we are children of God and seated with Christ in heavenly places (see Eph. 2:6). From that position in Christ, we have authority over the kingdom of darkness. Every believer is alive in Christ and therefore united with Him:

In His death—Romans 6:3; Galatians 2:20; Colossians 3:1-3;

In His burial—Romans 6:4;

In His resurrection—Romans 6:5,8,11;

In His ascension—Ephesians 2:6;

In His life—Romans 5:10-11;

In His power—Ephesians 1:19-20;

In His inheritance—Romans 8:16-17; Ephesians 1:11-12.

ANXIETY AS A BATTLE FOR THE MIND

Anxiety is fear without an apparent cause. Fear is not the same as anxiety, in that fear is actually identified by its object. For instance, we might fear other people, death, snakes or enclosed places.

Many people are paralyzed by fears that seem to be irrational to others who do not see or question the existence of the object of the fear. When people fear something that others cannot hear or see, we usually say that they are suffering a panic, or anxiety, attack.

These cases often prove to be spiritual battles for the mind. Remember, we wrestle "not against flesh and blood" (Eph. 6:12). In other words, our enemy does not materialize in the physical realm because the battle is spiritual. It is also very real.

The Origin of Our Thoughts

It is critical to distinguish between deceiving thoughts from the enemy and thoughts that are truly ours. If we think that tempting or accusing thoughts are our own, then we are going to reach some very bad conclusions about ourselves. God does not tempt us, but the devil will. "Let no one say when he is tempted, 'I am being tempted by God'; for God cannot be tempted by evil, and He Himself does not tempt anyone" (Jas. 1:13). Jesus will never accuse you, because there is "no condemnation for those who are in Christ Jesus" (Rom. 8:1). But the devil "deceives the whole world" (Rev. 12:9) and accuses believers day and night (see v. 10).

A very mature Christian girl discovered that she had cancer. Her doctors immediately treated her with chemotherapy. Then she became fearful. When I (Neil) visited with her, she said, "I'm not sure if I am a Christian." I asked her why she would even question her salvation, and she said, "When I go to church I have these blasphemous thoughts go through my mind, and many times I struggle with evil and perverted thoughts."

"That's not you!" I told her. "Scripture teaches that you 'joy-fully concur with the law of God in the inner man'" (Rom. 7:22).

If such thoughts originated from the girl herself, then what would she logically conclude about herself? She reasoned, *If those thoughts were actually coming from my own nature, then I must not be a Christian.* Consequently, she was frightened about the prospect of dying. After all, how can a Christian think those kinds of thoughts? Any Christian can *choose* to think them, but these thoughts do not originate from anyone who is in Christ. Because of this girl's maturity, I was able to help her get rid of those thoughts within an hour. She never questioned her salvation again.

False Identity or True?

Every Christian has thoughts about sin, but many do not under-stand the battle for their minds. Suppose a young man had a sexually tempting thought about another man. At first he might be a little surprised and would probably just brush it off. He cer-tainly would not tell anybody. If the thought persisted, he might start wondering why. *If I am thinking these thoughts, then maybe I am homosexual,* he might wonder. If so, he just bought a false identi-ty, and it could be years, if ever, before he shares what went on in his mind. People struggling with depression are plagued with lots of thoughts that are not true.

True mental health is characterized by "the peace of God, which surpasses all comprehension [guarding] your hearts and your minds in Christ Jesus" (Phil. 4:7). It begins with a true knowledge of our heavenly Father and a true knowledge of who we are in Christ. If you knew and believed that

- your heavenly Father loved you (see Eph. 3:14-19);
- you now have eternal life in Christ (see John 3:16);
- you are spiritually alive right now (see 1 John 5:11);

- He would never leave nor forsake you (see Heb. 13:5);
- He has completely forgiven you (see Col. 2:13-14);
- He would supply all your needs (see Phil. 4:19);
- you were a child of God (see Rom. 8:16);
- there was no condemnation for those who are in Christ Jesus (see Rom. 8:1);
- you have an eternal purpose for being here (see Eph. 2:10);
- you can do all things through Christ who strengthens you (see Phil. 4:13);
- God has not given you a spirit of fear but of power and love and discipline (see 2 Tim. 1:7);
- the peace of God was guarding your heart and your mind in Christ Jesus (see Phil. 4:7);

then you would have the foundational beliefs necessary to establish mental, emotional and spiritual health.

Mental Strongholds

Believing thoughts and feelings about ourselves that are not true inevitably establishes mental strongholds. Do not get the impression that all the lies we have learned to believe about ourselves and God come directly from Satan. The world and the flesh are also enemies of the soul. Most false beliefs about ourselves and God come from living in a fallen world. They are patterns of the flesh that can only be changed by renewing our minds through the truth of God's Word.

Taking Our Thoughts Captive

In one sense, it does not matter whether a thought comes from our memory bank, the television set, another person, Satan or our own creativity. The answer to what we are to do about it is always the same. Regardless of its origin, we are to take "*every*

Regardless of its origin, we are to take "every thought captive to the obedience of Christ."

thought captive to the obedience of Christ" (2 Cor. 10:5, emphasis added). If what we think is not true or edifying, then we should not think it.

Telling people just to stop thinking negative thoughts is not a complete answer. We overcome negative thinking by choosing to think and believe the truth. As Paul says in Philippians 4:8 (*NIV*): "Finally, brothers, whatever is *true*, whatever is noble, whatever is right, whatever is pure, whatever is lovely, whatever is admirable—if anything is excellent or praiseworthy—*think* about such things" (emphasis added). In other words, *we are not called to dispel the darkness; we are called to turn on the light.*

It is our experience that we can win the battle for our minds if we are free in Christ. But we cannot win if we have many unresolved personal and spiritual conflicts. Paul drives this point home in 1 Corinthians 3:2-3, when he tells Christians at Corinth that they were not able to receive the truth because of the jealousy and quarrels among them.

That is why when we work with teens, our first step is to help them resolve their conflicts through a process of repentance, which includes submitting to God and resisting the devil (see

Jas. 4:7). *Establishing* freedom in Christ and *staying* free are different issues, however. We maintain our freedom as we continue to believe the truth and live by faith. After giving us that list of what to think about in Philippians 4:8, Paul continues in verse 9 (*NIV*), "Whatever you have learned or received or heard from me, or seen in me—put it into practice. And the God of peace will be with you."

You are not alone in your struggle to manage your thoughts. Every believer has to contend with the world, the flesh and the devil.

Lies We Often Believe

The following statements are some of the most common lies that depressed teens tend to believe about themselves, life in general and their relationships with God:

- I'm worthless and would be better off dead.
- I have no value and no meaningful purpose in life.
- I'll never amount to anything.
- No one loves me or cares about me.
- My situation is hopeless. I see no way out but to die.
- I'm stupid! I'm ugly!
- I'm a mistake!
- God doesn't love me and He won't help me.
- Life is the pits.
- My future is hopeless.
- Nobody can help me.

The list could continue with many other blasphemous thoughts about God and negative thoughts about the teens themselves and others.

Nobody is going to fix the past. Not even God will do that. Nevertheless, the gospel assures us that we can be free from the past because we are not primarily products of the past. We are primarily products of Christ's work on the cross and His resurrection. Our primary identity is no longer in the flesh; it is in Christ. If that were not true, then all Christians would remain helpless victims of the past.

WEEDING OUT FALSE PERCEPTIONS

Realizing who we are in Christ and what it means to be a child of God is the basis for victorious living and an essential basis for overcoming depression. People cannot consistently behave in a way that is inconsistent with how they perceive themselves, nor can their feelings about themselves be any different from their perceptions about themselves.

For example, we will struggle with a poor self-image to the degree that we do not see ourselves the way God sees us. Such negative perceptions of ourselves are based on lies we have believed. They are like weeds in a field of grain. They stunt the growth of the good seed and rob the harvest. "Whatever a man sows, this he will also reap. For the one who sows to his own flesh shall from the flesh reap corruption, but the one who sows to the Spirit shall from the Spirit reap eternal life" (Gal. 6:7-8). If we sow a lie, we will reap corruption—garbage in, garbage out. We cannot plant weeds, hoping to reap a harvest of grain!

Truth or Consequences

Holding false perceptions about ourselves has some predictable consequences.

1. *False perceptions erode our confidence and weaken our resolve.* Many depressed people think they are losers and choose to believe they cannot do whatever it takes to overcome their problems. Of course, if they believe that lie, then they will not be able

to overcome anything. Failures fail, losers lose and sinners sin; but children of God live righteous lives and do all things through Christ who strengthens them.

In his first epistle, John writes, "Dear friends, now we are children of God. . . . Everyone who has this hope in him purifies himself, just as he is pure" (1 John 3:2-3, *NIV*). It is not what we do that determines who we are—it is who we are that determines what we do. That is why the Holy Spirit "bears witness with our spirit that we are children of God" (Rom. 8:16).

> Yet to all who received him, to those who believed in his name, he gave the right to become children of God—children born not of natural descent, nor of human decision or a husband's will, but born of God (John. 1:12-13, *NIV*).

2. *False perceptions drive us to seek our own acceptance, security and significance.* We try to accomplish this through appearance, performance and status. No matter how hard we try, we will still suffer from morbid introspection, hostile criticism, overt rejection and endless accusations. That is depressing! Acceptance, security and significance are already provided in Christ. Many young Christians are endlessly looking for what they already have in Christ. Others are desperately trying to become the people they already are. "Coming to Him as to a living stone, rejected by men, but choice and precious in the sight of God, you also, as living stones, are being built up as a spiritual house for a holy priesthood" (1 Pet. 2:4-5).

3. *False perceptions precipitate a fear of failure.* To stumble and fall is not failure. To stumble and fall again is not failure. Failure comes when you say you were pushed. When we blame others for our mistakes, we fail to see what we can do to prevent the mistake from happening again.

There are no unforgivable failures in the kingdom of God, but there are many people who live far below their potential because they have never learned the truth of who they are in Christ. "There is therefore now no condemnation for those who are in Christ Jesus" (Rom. 8:1).

We probably learn more from our mistakes than we will ever learn from our successes. A mistake is only a failure when we fail to learn from it. "For though a righteous man falls seven times, he rises again" (Prov. 24:16, *NIV*). If you make a mistake, get back up and try again—and again and again.

Depressed teens have a tendency to ask, "What do I stand to lose if I do try again?" They should ask, "What do I stand to lose if I don't?" This is not a question of self-confidence. Our confidence is in God. Paul said that we "worship in the Spirit of God and glory in Christ Jesus and put no confidence in the flesh" (Phil. 3:3).

4. *False perceptions cause us to seek the approval and affirmation of others.* The need for affirmation and approval is universal. This need is so great that it should draw us to our heavenly Father because we are not going to get the need perfectly met from people in this world, no matter how hard we try.

Jesus lived a perfect life, and everyone rejected Him. But He had the approval of His heavenly Father. Paul asks, "Am I now seeking the favor of men, or of God? Or am I striving to please men? If I were still trying to please men, I would not be a bond-servant of Christ" (Gal. 1:10). You will be a servant of humankind instead of a servant of God if you try to win the approval of others and seek their affirmation.

We cannot do things for God with the hope that He may some day accept us. We do those things because we already have His approval and affirmation in Christ. We do not labor in the vineyard with the hope that some day God may love us. We are already loved unconditionally by God because we are His children.

Scripture warns us not to exalt ourselves (see Luke 14:7-11), and to be aware of those who stroke our egos, "for such people are not serving our Lord Christ, but their own appetites. By smooth talk and flattery they deceive the minds of naive people" (Rom. 16:18, *NIV*).

Paul's written exhortation to the Thessalonians and to us is a reminder to be less concerned about the opinions of others and more concerned about what God thinks:

> We speak, not as pleasing men but God, who examines our hearts. For we never came with flattering speech, as you know, nor with a pretext for greed—God is witness— nor did we seek glory from men, either from you or from others" (1 Thess. 2:4-6).

5. *False perceptions rob us of the courage to stand up for our convictions and beliefs.* A person who has a low sense of self-worth thinks, *My opinions do not matter. If I share what I really believe, others will only squash me.* Caving in to the fear of rejection undermines the courage to stand up for our convictions.

Depressed teens frequently think of themselves as weak or cowardly. The book of Daniel records the story of three teenagers who stood against the cultural trends and mandates of their day. They refused to bow down to the golden image of Nebuchadnezzar, king of Babylon. He put himself on a pedestal as tall as a water tower—but Nebuchadnezzar was about to be knocked off.

Courageous acts of independence and the fortitude to hold true to your convictions are only possible with an inner confidence in God. Believers find their strength not in themselves but in the knowledge of who they are in Christ. "Finally, be strong in the Lord, and in the strength of His might" (Eph. 6:10).

6. *False perceptions lead to codependent relationships.* Every Christian is interdependent in a healthy sense because each of us needs God and each other. We are under the conviction of God to love one another. Relationships become unhealthy, however, when we begin to think, *I cannot live without you, your acceptance or your approval.*

The intense desire to have our emotional needs met by other people can often lead to compromising our own standards and values.

7. *False perceptions make it difficult to receive ordinary compliments.* Affirmations, praise and compliments do not remove the terrible pain that depressed people feel. Because the pain did not go away with an expression of praise or gratitude, a depressed person wrongly concludes that the kind words were not genuine.

Acceptance and affirmation accomplish more when directed toward the person's character and when the words reinforce who he or she really is in Christ. On the other hand, rejection and criticism of any kind, even unintentional, contribute to the depressed state of an insecure person. He or she will likely match such comments with his or her existing false perceptions.

INADEQUATE SOLUTIONS

We cannot think of topics that produce a bigger and more tangled mess with more inadequate solutions than the topics of identity and self-esteem. The world has a lot of things that sound good but cannot deliver when it comes to true freedom in Christ, and struggling young people deserve to be warned of these less-than-adequate approaches.

Secular approaches will have us pick ourselves up by our own bootstraps and stroke one another's egos. This, however, clearly does not meet our needs.

Even among Christians we hear many inadequate solutions. It has been suggested that a man should derive most of his identity from his work and a woman should get hers from bearing children.

But these are *fallen* identities. What happens if the man loses his job? Does he lose his identity? What happens if a woman never marries or cannot give birth to children? Does she lose her identity? In creation and through redemption, God has already established who we are.

If the "traditional" source of getting our identity is misplaced, then from where should our self-worth come?

Spiritual Gifts?

Do we get a sense of worth from spiritual gifts? No! Right in the middle of the most definitive teaching about spiritual gifts, Paul says:

> Those members of the body, which we deem less honorable, on these we bestow more abundant honor, and our unseemly members come to have more abundant seemliness, whereas our seemly members have no need of it. But God has so composed the body, giving more abundant honor to that member which lacked (1 Cor. 12:23-24).

Talents?

Do we get our sense of worth from talents? No! God has given some of us one talent, some two and others five (see Matt. 25:14-30). We might ask, "God, how could you do that? Don't You know, Lord, that only the five-talent person could have any legitimate sense of worth?" That is not true. In fact, supergifted and talented people often struggle more because they attempt to find their worth in their talents, drawing attention to themselves rather than using their gifts to edify the Body of Christ, the Church. The attempt can also distract that person from developing his character and relationship with God, which is the source of true fulfillment.

Intelligence?

Surely our sense of worth must come from intelligence. No! "God has chosen the foolish things of the world to shame the wise" (1 Cor. 1:27). God has not distributed intelligence equally any more than He has given out the same number of gifts and talents. He has, however, *equally distributed Himself.* Only in Christ is there equality:

> You are all sons of God through faith in Christ Jesus. For all of you who were baptized into Christ have clothed yourself with Christ. There is neither Jew nor Greek, there is neither slave nor free man, there is neither male nor female; for you are all one in Christ Jesus. And if you belong to Christ, then you are Abraham's offspring, heirs according to promise (Gal. 3:26-29).

Our identity and sense of self-worth come from knowing who we are as children of God and then becoming the people He created us to be.

Appearance, Performance or Social Status?

Perhaps the most fickle of all false foundations of self-worth are appearance, performance and social status. A fallen humanity labors under the following wrong equations:

APPEARANCE + ADMIRATION = A WHOLE PERSON

PERFORMANCE + ACCOMPLISHMENTS = A WHOLE PERSON

SOCIAL STATUS + RECOGNITION = A WHOLE PERSON

Recognition is not the same as acceptance, and the respect given by others may be more for the position than the person. No matter how hard we try, someone will come along and look better or outperform us. Talents and appearances also fade with time. When we strive for the acceptance, recognition or admiration of others, then *they* determine our worth. If they judge us unworthy, are we then worthless?

What a tragedy occurs when we put our identity and sense of self-esteem in someone else's hands. Who is qualified to judge our worth? Who has the right to declare us to have value? Will a pot declare another pot seemly or unseemly? Only the Potter has the right to determine who we are. The value He placed on our lives cost Him His only begotten Son. The true equation is

YOU + CHRIST = YOU AS A WHOLE PERSON

Certainly nothing is wrong with having gifts, talents, intelligence and appearance. They are life endowments given to us by our Creator. We are to be good stewards of such gifts. But if someone endowed us with a new car, we would not find our identity and sense of worth in the car. We hope we would understand that the giver had already found value in us and that is why he gave us the car. And even though no strings were attached to the gift, we would want to use the car in a way that would show appreciation for the gift. To abuse the free gift would be to insult the giver.

THE ONLY ANSWER—CHRIST

Our identity and sense of worth come from knowing who we are as children of God and then becoming the people He created us to be. Nobody and nothing on Earth can keep you from being that, because it is God's will for your life. "For this is the will of God, your sanctification" (1 Thess. 4:3).

If, as Christians, we knew who we were in Christ and if our lives were characterized by love, joy, peace, patience, kindness, goodness, faithfulness, gentleness and self-control, would we feel good about ourselves? Of course we would! Who can have that sense of self-worth? Every child of God has exactly the same opportunity, because those traits are the fruit of the Spirit (see Gal. 5:22-23), of which every Christian is a partaker.

Such characteristics cannot come by way of the world, the flesh or the devil. They can only come by abiding in Christ and by walking by faith and in the power of the Holy Spirit according to what God says is true.

Paul says, "My God shall supply all your needs according to His riches in glory in Christ Jesus" (Phil. 4:19). Our material needs are minimal. The most critical needs that must be met are the "being" needs, and they are the ones most wonderfully met in Christ.

The greatest need is life itself, and Jesus came that we might have life. Then there is the need to know who we are, and the Spirit bears witness with our spirit that we are children of God. Finally, we need to feel accepted, secure and significant. We wrote *Stomping Out the Darkness* and a devotional called *Extreme Faith* to show how those needs can only be met in Christ. The verses from the Bible found in the appendix reveal who we are and how our needs are met.

DEPRESSION BUSTERS

Read:

Ephesians 6:10-16

Reflect:

1. Why, in most people's lives, is depression *primarily* a software (mental programming) problem, rather than a hardware (brain) problem?
2. In some ways all of us experience a battle for our minds. In what ways have you personally experienced a spiritual attack in your mind? How are you taking those thoughts captive?
3. List the seven ways that we as believers are united with Christ that we covered in this chapter?
4. What are the seven false perceptions that young people might have about themselves?
5. Read through the "Who I Am in Christ" list in the appendix and select at least one verse to memorize.

Respond:

Dear Lord, You said, "Finally, be strong in the Lord and in the strength of His might. Put on the full armor of God, that you may be able to stand firm against the devil's schemes. For our struggle is not against flesh and blood, but against the rulers, against the powers, against the world forces of this darkness, against the spiritual forces of wickedness in the heavenly places.

Therefore, take up the full armor of God, that you may be able to resist in the evil day" (Eph. 6:11, NIV). Lord, I choose to put on this armor, every piece of it, that it might destroy depression and hopelessness in my life. In Jesus' name I pray. Amen.

Note
1. Janis Whipple, "Washed Away," *DevoZine* November/December 1997, n.p.

CHAPTER 8

OVERCOMING HOPELESSNESS—THE BELLY OF THE BEAST

Why are you downcast, O my soul? Why so disturbed within me? Put your hope in God, for I will yet praise him, my Savior and my God.

PSALM 42:5-6, *NIV*

If you lose the power to laugh, you lose the power to think.

CLARENCE DARROW

The psalmist is not only depressed, but he is also in deep despair. He is overwhelmed by a sense of hopelessness. The hopelessness that comes with depression was described by one girl who said, "It feels like I am in a well 1,000 feet deep. From the bottom I look up and see a faint light the size of a pinhole. I have no ladder, no rope and no way out."

THE LIE OF HOPELESSNESS

The hopelessness of depression is based on a lie. With God there is always hope, and that hope is based on truth. However, when we are bound by the chains of hopelessness, this seems too good to be true. Consider the following parable:

A newly adopted child found himself in a big mansion. His new father whispered in his ear, "This is yours and you have a right to be here. I have made you a joint heir with my only-begotten son. He paid the price that set you free from your old taskmaster, who was cruel and condemning. I purchased it for you because I love you."

The young boy couldn't help but question this incredible gift. *This seems too good to be true. What did I do to deserve this?* he wondered. *I have been a slave all my life and I have done nothing to earn such a privilege!*

He was deeply grateful, however, and began to explore all the rooms in the mansion. He tried out some of the tools and appliances. Many other adopted people also lived in the mansion, and the boy began to form new relationships with his adopted brothers and sisters.

He especially enjoyed the buffet from which he freely ate. Then it happened! While turning away from the buffet table, he knocked over a stack of glasses and a valuable pitcher. They crashed to the floor and broke. Instantly he thought, *You clumsy, stupid kid! You will never get away with this. What right do you have to be here? You better hide before someone finds out, because they will surely throw you out.*

At first he was caught up with the wonder of living in the mansion with a new family and a loving father, but now he was confused. Old tapes laid down in early childhood began to play again in his mind. He was filled with guilt and shame. The self-condemning thoughts continued. *Who do you think you are, some kind of a privileged character? You don't belong here, you belong in the basement! My old taskmaster was right about me—I don't belong here.* As his mind filled with these thoughts, the boy descended into the cellar.

The basement was dreary, dark and despairing. The only light came from the open door at the top of the long stairs from which he had come. He heard his new father calling for him, but he was too ashamed to answer.

The boy was surprised to find others in the basement. Upstairs everybody talked to each other and joined in with daily projects that were fun and meaningful. In the basement, however, nobody talked to each other. They were too ashamed. Although no one liked it there, most felt that the basement was where they really belonged. They didn't see how they could ever walk in the light again. If they did, others would see their imperfections.

Some of the people who lived upstairs would occasionally come to the door and encourage them to come back up where a place was prepared for them. Some "friends" were worse than others and would scold those in the basement, which only made it worse.

Not everyone stayed in the basement for the same reason. Some, like the boy, thought, *I deserve to be here. I was given a chance, but I blew it.* Others didn't think they could climb the stairs. Even if they mustered up the strength to try, the stairs would probably break under their weight. They always had a reason why they couldn't return to their father upstairs.

Some would gather the courage to go up for a short time, but they didn't stay long enough to resolve their conflicts and learn the truth that would enable them to stay. So they returned to the basement.

Still others were afraid that they would not be accepted. Their old taskmaster would not accept them, so how could they expect this adoptive parent to welcome them back after what they had done? Each had his own story about what he had done wrong.

At first, the newly adopted boy groped around in the darkness, trying to find a way to survive. The longer he stayed in the basement, the more the memory of what it was like to live upstairs began to fade, along with his hope of ever returning. Those old tapes from early childhood questioned the love of this new father, and he began to question whether he was ever adopted in the first place.

The noise of people having fun upstairs irritated him. He remembered the light in the house being warm and inviting, but now, whenever the basement door opened, the light seemed penetrating and revealing. He recalled hearing his adopted father saying that most people loved the darkness rather than the light, for their deeds were evil.

The boy made a few half-hearted attempts to return to the light, but eventually he found a dark corner and lay down in it. To survive, he ate grubs and moss off the damp walls.

Then one day a shaft of light penetrated his mind, and reason returned. He began to think, *Why not throw myself on the mercy of this person who calls himself my father? What do I have to lose? Even if he makes me eat the crumbs that fall from the table, it would be better than this.* So he decided to take the risk of climbing those stairs and facing his father with the truth of what he had done.

"Father," he said, "I knocked over some glasses and broke a pitcher." Without saying a word, his father took him by the hand and led him into the dining room. To the boy's utter amazement, his father had prepared a banquet for him!

"Welcome home, Son," his father said. "There is no condemnation for those who are in my family!"

Oh, the deep, deep love of Jesus and the matchless grace of God! The door is always open for those who are willing to throw themselves upon His mercy. "In love He predestined us to adop-

If people could accept our heavenly Father's grace and love, they would never confine themselves in the basement of depression or the grip of hopelessness.

tion as sons through Jesus Christ to Himself, according to the kind intention of His will, to the praise of the glory of His grace, which He freely bestowed on us in the Beloved" (Eph. 1:4-6). If people could accept our heavenly Father's grace and love, they would never confine themselves in the basement of depression or the grip of hopelessness.

Our heavenly Father does not want us to live self-condemned in the basement. He wants us to know that we are seated with Christ in heavenly places as joint heirs with Jesus. "Now if we are children, then we are heirs—heirs of God and co-heirs with Christ, if indeed we share in his sufferings in order that we may also share in his glory" (Rom. 8:17, *NIV*).

ACCEPTING GOD'S GRACE

How can we help a depressed person understand the love and grace of God? How can *anyone* fully understand it? Everything we have learned in the world has taught us that life is a jungle and that only people who are mentally, emotionally and physically fit enough will survive. We learn that justice demands that we get what we deserve. It strikes a discordant note when we hear: "But when the kindness of God our Savior and His love for mankind appeared, He saved us, not on the basis of deeds which we have done in righteousness, but according to His mercy" (Titus 3:4-5).

Inspired by the Holy Spirit, Paul offers two prayers in the book of Ephesians. He first asks God to open the eyes of Christians to who we are and what we have in Christ.

I pray that the eyes of your heart may be enlightened, so that you may know what is the hope of His calling, what are the riches of the glory of His inheritance in the saints, and what is the surpassing greatness of His power toward us who believe (Eph. 1:18-19).

In the second passage, Paul approaches God on our behalf. Personalize this prayer by putting your name in the spaces allotted:

> *For this reason, I bow my knees before the Father, from whom every family in heaven and on Earth derives its name, that He would grant _____, according to the riches of His glory, to be strengthened with power through His Spirit in _____'s inner man; so that Christ may dwell in _____'s heart through faith; and that _____, being rooted and grounded in love, may be able to comprehend with all the saints what is the breadth and length and height and depth, and to know the love of Christ which surpasses knowledge, that _____ may be filled up to all the fullness of God (see Eph. 3:14-19).*
> *"[God] made Him who knew no sin to be sin on [my] behalf, that [I] might become the righteousness of God in Him" (2 Cor. 5:21).*
> *I cannot do for myself what Christ has already done for me. "For by grace [I] have been saved through faith; and that not of [myself], it is the gift of God; not as a result of works, that no one should boast" (Eph. 2:8-9). In Jesus' name I pray. Amen.*

Turning Down God's Gift

Some people refuse to accept this free gift of life, because they do not feel worthy. But understand that such a rejection is not true humility. Instead, it will lead to defeat and hopelessness.

Many people have then reasoned, *I believe that Jesus died for the sins I have already committed, but what about the sins I commit in the future? What if I broke the glasses and the pitcher after I was invited to live with my new family?* When Christ "died to sin, once for all"

(Rom. 6:10), how many of your sins were still to happen in the future? All of them were! This is not a license to go on sinning. It is a glorious truth that enables us to know that we are truly forgiven and can now live a righteous life because we are "dead to sin, but alive to God in Christ Jesus" (v. 11).

Without the grace of God and Christ's death on the cross, we *would* be guilty and we could do nothing about it. Every attempt to live a righteous life in our own strength would fail. But the penalty for the sins of the world has been paid in full, and the payment is applied to our account when we trust in Christ.

Then why do so many of us feel so guilty? After we receive forgiveness of sins, guilt is just a feeling based on a lie or a humanly developed conscience—in which case the guilt is only psychological. The conscience is a part of the mind and is not the same as the convicting work of the Holy Spirit. Even nonbelievers have a conscience, and they will feel shame or guilt when they violate it.

The process of renewing the mind will bring the conscience in conformity to the nature and character of God. The devil first tempts us to sin. Then, as soon as we make a mistake, he becomes the accuser, saying "You will never get away with this" or "How can you even consider yourself a Christian if you do those kinds of things?" But the Lord has forgiven our sins and defeated the devil, as Paul so clearly reveals:

And when you were dead in your transgressions and the uncircumcision of your flesh, He made you alive together with Him, having forgiven us all our transgressions, having canceled out the certificate of debt consisting of decrees against us and which was hostile to us; and He has taken it out of the way, having nailed it to the cross. When He had disarmed the rulers and authorities, He made a public display of them, having triumphed over them through Him (Col. 2:13-15).

Discerning Truth and Lies

The Lord will not tempt us, but He will test us to perfect our faith. He will also convict us of sin to cleanse us from all unrighteousness. How then do we know the difference between the convicting work of the Holy Spirit, and the accusations of the devil or a condemning conscience that has been programmed by the world? Paul gives one answer in 2 Corinthians 7:9-10:

> I now rejoice, not that you were made sorrowful, but that you were made sorrowful to the point of repentance; for you were made sorrowful according to the will of God. . . . For the sorrow that is according to the will of God produces a repentance without regret, leading to salvation; but the sorrow of the world produces death.

The word "sorrow" is used to refer to both the convicting that comes from God as well as the false guilt produced by the world, the flesh and the devil. Both experiences may feel the same, but the end result is totally different. The conviction God sends us leads to repentance without regret.

This is a wonderful truth we have witnessed many times. I have never seen any teenager regret going through the Steps to Freedom in Christ and resolving their personal and spiritual conflicts through repentance and faith in God. What stays with the teen afterward is the freedom he or she achieved, not the pain from the past. It was nailed to the Cross.

Peter betrayed Christ by denying Him three times. Later he came under the conviction of the Holy Spirit and became a spokesperson for the Early Church. Judas betrayed Christ, came under the sorrow of the world and hanged himself.

NOT LIVING UP TO THE GOOD NEWS

During the American Civil War, General Sherman burned Atlanta and then waged terror against the civilians of the South during his long march toward the Atlantic coast. His theory was that soldiers fight wars but that civilians support the soldiers and pay for war. He wanted to defeat the South's ability to support the battle. He broke the back of the war effort the moment the civilians felt defeated, hopeless, useless and helpless and no longer believed the conflict could be won.

This is exactly what Satan wants us to believe. He wants us to be demoralized in the spiritual battle between good and evil. But our war with the world, the flesh and the devil has already been won! We just have to believe it.

Slavery in the United States was abolished on December 18, 1865, by the Thirteenth Amendment to the Constitution. How many slaves were there on December 19? In reality, none; but many still lived like slaves—because they had not learned the truth. Others knew and even believed that they were free but chose to live as they had been taught under slavery.

Several plantation owners were devastated by this proclamation of emancipation. "We're ruined!" they cried. "Slavery has been abolished. We've lost the battle to keep our slaves." But Satan, the chief spokesman against the truth, slyly responded, "Not necessarily. As long as these people *think* they're still slaves, the Emancipation Proclamation will have no practical effect. We don't have a legal right over them anymore, but many of them don't know it. Keep your slaves from learning the truth, and your control over them will not even be challenged."

"But, what if the news spreads?"

"Don't panic. We have another bullet to fire. We may not be able to keep them from hearing the news, but we can still keep them from understanding it. They don't call me the father of lies for nothing. We still have the potential to deceive the whole world. Just tell them that they misunderstood the Thirteenth Amendment. Tell them that they are going to be free, not that they are free already. The truth they heard is just positional truth, not actual truth. Someday they may receive the benefits but not now."

"But they'll expect us to say that. They won't believe us."

"Then pick out a few persuasive ones who are convinced that they're still slaves, and let them do the talking for you. Remember, most of these free people were born slaves and have lived like slaves all their lives. All we have to do is to deceive them so that they still think like slaves. As long as they continue to do what slaves do, it will not be hard to convince them that they must still be slaves. They will maintain their slave identity because of the things they do. The moment they try to profess that they are no longer slaves, just whisper in their ears, 'How can you even think you are no longer a slave when you are still doing things that slaves do?' After all, we have the capacity to accuse the brethren day and night."

Years later, many people still had not heard the wonderful news that they had been freed, so they continued to live the way they had always lived. Some had heard the good news, but they evaluated it according to what they were doing and feeling. They reasoned, *I'm still living in bondage, doing the same things I have always done. My experience tells me that I must not be free. I'm feeling the same way I was before the proclamation, so it must not be true. After all, our feelings always tell the truth.* So they continued to live according to how they felt, not wanting to be hypocrites!

One former slave hears the good news and receives it with great joy. He checks out the validity of the proclamation and

The gospel is the Emancipation Proclamation for all sinners.

finds out that the highest of all authorities has originated the decree. Not only that, but it personally cost that authority a tremendous price, which he willingly paid, so that the slave could be free. His life is transformed. He correctly reasons that it would be hypocritical to believe his feelings and not believe the truth. Determined to live by what he knows to be true, his experiences begin to change rather dramatically. He realizes that his old master has no authority over him and does not need to be obeyed. He gladly serves the one who set him free.[1]

The gospel is the Emancipation Proclamation for all sinners. Because of the Fall, we were all enslaved to sin. We were dead in our "trespasses and sins" (Eph. 2:1) "and were by nature children of wrath" (v. 3). The good news is that we are no longer slaves to sin. We are now alive in Christ and dead to sin (see Rom. 6:11). We have been set free in Christ. We are not sinners in the hands of an angry God. We are saints in the hands of a loving God. We are forgiven, justified, redeemed and born-again children of God.

You may not feel like it, you may not act like it, and others may tell you that you are not, but you have been justified in Christ. "Therefore having been justified by faith, we have peace with God through our Lord Jesus Christ" (Rom. 5:1).

TAKING GOD AT HIS WORD

According to Hebrews 6:13-20 (*NIV*), God stakes His own credibility on the fact that our hope is in Him:

> When God made his promise to Abraham, since there was no one greater for him to swear by, he swore by himself, saying, "I will surely bless you and give you many descendants." And so after waiting patiently, Abraham received what was promised. Men swear by someone greater than themselves, and the oath confirms what is said and puts an end to all argument. Because God wanted to make the unchanging nature of his purpose very clear to the heirs of what was promised, he confirmed it with an oath. God did this so that, by two unchangeable things in which it is impossible for God to lie, we who have fled to take hold of the hope offered to us may be greatly encouraged. We have this hope as an anchor for the soul, firm and secure. It enters the inner sanctuary behind the curtain, where Jesus, who went before us, has entered on our behalf.

Two unchangeable things are God's promise and the oath confirming the promise. Our hope in God is a solid anchor for our souls, and He is the answer to hopelessness and depression. If God cannot lie, then the basis for our hope is found in the truth of His nature, character and Word.

Hopelessness from Faulty Perceptions

Although God cannot change, our perception of Him can. Such a change will greatly affect how we feel. To illustrate this, look at how Jeremiah became depressed because his perceptions about God were all wrong:

I am the man who has seen affliction because of the rod of His wrath. He has driven me and made me walk in darkness and not in light. Surely against me He has turned His hand repeatedly all the day. He has caused my flesh and my skin to waste away, He has broken my bones. He has besieged and encompassed me with bitterness and hardship. In dark places He has made me dwell, like those who have long been dead (Lam. 3:1-6).

Jeremiah believed that God was the cause of his physical and emotional hardships. He actually thought that God was out to get him, when in fact He was out to restore him. Instead of being led by God, Jeremiah felt that he was being driven to dark places where God had abandoned him. Jeremiah was in the basement! Read his feelings of entrapment, hopelessness and fear:

He has walled me in so that I cannot go out; He has made my chain heavy. Even when I cry out and call for help, He shuts out my prayer. He has blocked my ways with hewn stone; He has made my paths crooked. He is to me like a bear lying in wait, like a lion in secret places. He has turned aside my ways and torn me to pieces; He has made me desolate. So I say, "My strength has perished, and so has my hope from the LORD" (Lam. 3:18).

Jeremiah was depressed because his perception of God was wrong. God was not the cause of his affliction. God did not set up the circumstances to make his life miserable. God is not a wild beast waiting to chew up people. But Jeremiah thought He was, and consequently he lost all hope in God. Then suddenly everything changed:

I remember my affliction and my wandering, the bitterness and the gall. I well remember them, and my soul is downcast within me. Yet this I call to mind and therefore I have hope: Because of the LORD's great love we are not consumed, for his compassions never fail. They are new every morning; great is your faithfulness. I say to myself, "The LORD is my portion; therefore I will wait for him." The LORD is good to those whose hope is in him, to the one who seeks him; it is good to wait quietly for the salvation of the LORD (Lam. 3:19-26, *NIV*).

Nothing had changed externally in Jeremiah's experience. The only thing that had changed was his perception of God. He had won the battle for his mind by recalling what he knew to be true about God. Hope returns when we choose to believe in the true nature and character of God.

This is why it is so necessary for us to worship God. Our heavenly Father is not an egomaniac who needs His ego stroked every Sunday morning. He is totally secure within Himself. He does not need us to tell Him who He is. We worship God because we need to keep the divine attributes of God constantly on our minds. We do not worship God to change Him; we worship God to change ourselves, as Jeremiah did.

DEPRESSION BUSTERS

Read:

Ephesians 1:18-19

Reflect:

1. Why is accepting our heavenly Father's grace and love so important when it comes to overcoming depression?
2. What would you do to help a depressed person understand the grace of God and how would you help that person overcome the lies that he or she has learned from the world?
3. Some people refuse to accept this free gift of life that Jesus offers because they do not feel worthy. Why is this both false humility and a sure road to defeat and hopelessness?
4. What are two unchangeable qualities of God?
5. Why is having a proper perception of God so important when it comes to overcoming depression?

Respond:

Dear Lord, I, like Paul, pray that the eyes of my heart might be enlightened so that I may know what is the hope of Your calling, the riches of the glory of Your inheritance in the saints and the surpassing greatness of Your power toward me, because I believe and trust in You. Lord, I know that You are the God of hope and that at times I have lived a hopeless life. I turn from my hopelessness and turn to You. I, like Jeremiah, have not always thought and believed the truth about You. Thank You for forgiving me, setting me straight and giving me hope again. In Jesus' name I pray. Amen.

Notes

1. Neil T. Anderson, *Living Free in Christ* (Ventura, CA: Regal Books, 1993), pp. 56-58.

CHAPTER 9

OVERCOMING HELPLESSNESS—INTO THE LIGHT

I lift up my eyes to the hills—where does my help come from? My help comes from the LORD, the Maker of heaven and earth.

PSALM 121:1-2, *NIV*

When we live in joy, the virtue of joy, we live in the Kingdom of God.

MEGAN MCKENNA

Do you sometimes feel helpless and useless? Do you sometimes think you have no good qualities or redeeming value as a person? As children of God we still have weaknesses and flaws but our value never changes as this next story shows us.

A water bearer in India had two large pots, each hung on each end of a pole which he carried across his neck. One of the pots had a crack in it, and all the other pots were perfect and always delivered a full portion of water at the end of the long walk from the stream to the master's house, the cracked pot arrived half full.

For a full two years, this went on daily, with the bearer delivering only one and a half pots full of water to his master's house. Of course, the perfect pot was proud of its accomplishments . . . perfect to the end for which it was made. But the poor, cracked pot was ashamed of its own imperfection, and miserable that it was able to accomplish only half of what it had been made to do.

After two years of what it perceived to be a bitter failure, it spoke to the water bearer one day by the stream. "I am ashamed of myself, and I want to apologize to you."

"Why?" asked the bearer. "What are you ashamed of?"

"I have been able, for these past two years, to deliver only half my load because this crack in my side causes water to leak out all the way back to your master's house. Because of my flaws, you have to do all of this work, and you don't get full value from your efforts," the pot said.

The water bearer felt sorry for the old, cracked pot, and in his compassion he said, "As we return to the master's house, I want you to notice the beautiful flowers along the path."

Indeed, as they went up the hill, the old, cracked pot took notice of the sun warming the beautiful wildflowers on the side of the path, and the scene cheered it some. But at the end of the trail, the pot still felt bad because it had leaked out half its load, and so again, the pot apologized to the bearer for its failure.

The bearer said to the pot, "If you notice that there were flowers only on your side of the path, but not on the other pot's side? That's because I have always known about your flaw, and I took advantage of it. I planted flower seeds on your side of the path, and every day while we walk back from the stream, you've watered them. For two years I have been able to pick these beautiful flowers to decorate my master's table. Without you being just the way you are, he would have not had this beauty to grace his house."

Each of us has our own unique flaws to grace His Father's table. In God's great economy, nothing goes to waste. Don't be afraid of your flaws. Acknowledge them, and you too can be the cause of beauty. Know that in our weakness we find our strength.[1]

Teenagers who struggle with depression frequently complain about feelings of helplessness. They point to a series of life circumstances which are beyond their control. These often include job loss, death of a loved one, parents' divorce and serious illness or injury. Because they have no control over these events, they begin to believe that they are inadequate, incompetent and powerless. Consequently, they feel helpless. Although the Bible declares they can do all things through Christ who strengthens them (see Phil. 4:13), they are overwhelmed by the belief that they are unable to affect their world or keep from being overtaken by it!

God did not create His children helpless or emotionally paralyzed. Helplessness creeps in when we do not know or do not believe the truth. Helplessness is something we learn. It is very hard to unlearn.

As Grasshoppers in Their Own Eyes

The Israelites had been enslaved in Egypt for 400 years when God revealed to Moses His plans to set them free. God challenged Moses:

> Therefore, say to the Israelites: "I am the LORD, and I will bring you out from under the yoke of the Egyptians. I will free you from being slaves to them, and I will redeem you with an outstretched arm and with mighty acts of judgment. I will take you as my own people, and I will be your God. Then you will know that I am the LORD your God, who brought you out from under the yoke of the Egyptians. And I will bring you to the land I swore with uplifted hand to give to Abraham, to Isaac and to Jacob. I will give it to you as a possession. I am the LORD" (Exod. 6:6-8, NIV).

Pack your bags, Israelites! God is about to set you free! He knows your plight. He loves you, and He wants to redeem you and bring you back to the land of your dreams.

But look at the Israelites' response to this good news: "Moses reported this to the Israelites, but they did not listen to him because of their discouragement and cruel bondage" (v. 9, NIV). Years of conditioning created in the Israelites a sense of learned helplessness, even when God Himself said He would deliver them.

When God did deliver them, the people stalled in the wilderness. They became greatly discouraged and wanted to go back.

They rebelled and complained about Moses' leadership. About this time, "The LORD spoke to Moses saying, 'Send out for yourself men so that they may spy out the land of Canaan, which I am going to give to the sons of Israel; you shall send a man from each of their fathers' tribes, every one a leader among them'" (Num. 13:1-2). They came back to Moses and Aaron and the whole Israelite community and gave this report:

> "We went into the land to which you sent us, and it does flow with milk and honey! Here is its fruit. But the people who live there are powerful, and the cities are fortified and very large. We even saw descendants of Anak there." . . . Then Caleb silenced the people before Moses and said, "We should go up and take possession of the land, for we can certainly do it." But the men who had gone up with him said, "We can't attack those people; they are stronger than we are." And they spread among the Israelites a bad report about the land they had explored. They said, "The land we explored devours those living in it. All the people we saw there are of great size. We saw the Nephilim there (the descendants of Anak come from the Nephilim). We seemed like grasshoppers *in our own eyes*, and we looked the same to them" (Num. 13:27-33, *NIV*, emphasis added).

The people believed the bad report and rebelled against Moses and Aaron. But Joshua and Caleb said to the entire Israelite assembly:

> The land we passed through and explored is exceedingly good. If the LORD is pleased with us, he will lead us into that land, a land flowing with milk and honey, and will give it to us. Only do not rebel against the LORD. And do

not be afraid of the people of the land, because we will swallow them up. Their protection is gone, but the LORD is with us. Do not be afraid of them (Num. 14:7-9, *NIV*).

Unfortunately, the Israelites again believed the bad report, rather than the truth. The Lord delivered them into the Promised Land anyway, but because of their disobedience they would be delayed in the wilderness for another 40 years.

A GIANT OF A LIE AND A YOUTH WITH THE TRUTH

Even after they arrived in the land God gave them, the Israelites still encountered many obstacles. At one time, the Philistines challenged God's people to a winner-take-all match between their champion, Goliath, and anyone the Israelites chose. They were paralyzed by fear until David came along and said, "Who is this uncircumcised Philistine, that he should taunt the armies of the living God?" (1 Sam. 17:26). Then David said to Saul:

Let no man's heart fail on account of him [Goliath]; your servant will go and fight with this Philistine. . . . Your servant has killed both the lion and the bear; and this uncircumcised Philistine will be like one of them, since he has taunted the armies of the living God. . . . The LORD who delivered me from the paw of the lion and from the paw of the bear, He will deliver me from the hand of this Philistine (1 Sam. 17:32,36-37).

Even more impressive is what David said to the giant:

You come to me with sword, a spear, and a javelin, but I come to you in the name of the LORD of hosts, the God of the armies of Israel, whom you have taunted. This day the LORD will deliver you up into my hands, and I will strike you down and remove your head from you. And I will give the dead bodies of the army of the Philistines this day to the birds of the sky and the wild beasts of the earth, that all the earth may know that there is a God in Israel, and that all this assembly may know that the LORD does not deliver by sword or by spear; for the battle is the LORD's and He will give you into our hands (1 Sam. 17:45-47).

In their learned helplessness the Israelites saw the giant in relationship to themselves, whereas David saw him in relationship to God. The spies also saw the giants in the land in relationship to themselves, but Joshua and Caleb saw through the eyes of faith. They knew that the battle was the Lord's.

Just like the Israelites, when we reach God's promised land for each of us, we too will still face difficulties. Therefore, we must also see through eyes of faith if we are ever going to

In their learned helplessness the Israelites saw the giant in relationship to themselves, whereas David saw him in relationship to God.

experience any victory in this life. In Christ, God has given us the promised land. Jesus has pulled up the stakes that are keeping us immobilized. He has taken the glass partition away. God is with us, and nothing is impossible for Him. We can be like Joshua and Caleb and believe that we are never helpless with God, or we can be like those who choose to believe they are just as helpless now as they were before they believed in Christ.

ROOTS OF HELPLESSNESS

Most learned helplessness is the result of early childhood experiences. Lacking the presence of God in our lives and the knowledge of His ways, we learned how to survive by defending and protecting ourselves.

Many people have felt defeated at a very young age because the messages they received from the world were often negative:

It has been estimated that 95 percent of the world's population is pessimistic by nature. Even the weatherman says, "There will a 35 percent chance of rain tomorrow." He never says there will be a 65 percent chance of sunshine.

"You can't do that. You'd better let me do it." "You're not big enough or smart enough." "You'll never amount to anything." "It's a dog-eat-dog world out there, so be careful and watch your backside." Upon hearing these kinds of messages, it is no wonder that we start to believe *in our own helplessness*.

It has been estimated that 95 percent of the world's population is pessimistic by nature. Even the weatherman says, "There will a 35 percent chance of rain tomorrow." He never says there will be a 65 percent chance of sunshine. The news anchors rarely tell us about the good things that happened during the day—they mostly tell the bad news. Three news helicopters and 25 policemen will follow a fugitive in a car pursuit for hours, but nobody follows the good guy who spends his day encouraging others. What we see on the news distorts reality.

Blessing snatchers can be found everywhere. A teenager is likely to hear this from a friend or relative: "Oh, I see your parents bought you a new car. You know they will kill you if you wreck it." Even in churches, people are prone to point out the imminent dangers and the sad state of affairs in the world, rather than to encourage one another to live above difficult circumstances by having confidence in God. How many times has it been said: "I heard that you have just become a Christian. Congratulations—now you have an enemy you never had before"? The fact is now you have an all-powerful, loving God on your side!

OVERCOMING HELPLESSNESS

People in the world have told us what they think success is; yet no one can ever live up to that definition. Thankfully, God is not interested in the worldly version of success; rather, God focuses on our faithfulness. This next story illustrates our point.

One night a man was asleep in his cabin when he was suddenly awakened by the appearance of the Savior. His room was filled with light. The Lord said, "I have work for you to do." He showed the man a large rock, and told him to push against that rock with all his might. This the man did, and for many days he toiled from sunup to sundown, with his shoulder set squarely against the cold, massive surface of the rock, pushing with all his might. Each night the man returned to his cabin sore and worn out, wondering if his whole day had been spent in vain.

Seeing that the man was showing signs of discouragement, Satan decided to enter the picture. He placed thoughts in the man's mind, such as, "Why kill yourself over this project? You're never going to move that rock." Or "Boy! You've been at it a long time and you haven't even scratched the surface," etc., etc. The man began to get the impression that the task was impossible and that he was an unworthy servant because he wasn't able to move the massive stone.

These thoughts discouraged and disheartened him and he started to ease up on his efforts. "Why kill myself?" he thought. "I'll just put in my time, expending a minimum amount of effort and that will be good enough." And that he did, or at least planned on doing, until one day he decided to take his troubles to the Lord.

"Lord," he said, "I have labored hard and long in Your service, putting forth all my strength to do that which You have asked me. Yet, after all this time, I have not even nudged that rock half a millimeter. What is wrong? Am I failing You?"

"My son," the Lord answered, "when long ago I asked you to serve Me and you accepted, I told you to push against the rock with all your strength. That you have done. But never once did I mention that I expected you to move it, at least not by yourself! Your task was to push!

"Now you come to Me all discouraged, thinking that you have failed and ready to quit. But is that really so? Look at yourself. Your arms are strong and muscled; your back sinewed and brown. Your hands are calloused and your legs have become massive and hard. Through opposition you have grown much and your ability now far surpasses that which you used to have.

"Yet, you haven't succeeded in moving the rock; and you come to Me now with a heavy heart and your strength spent. I, My son, will move the rock. Your calling was to be obedient and to push, and to exercise your faith and trust in My wisdom. And this you have done."

We can do all things through Christ who strengthens us, but what *are* those "things"? In other words, what is God's will for our lives? Paul clearly tells us, "This is the will of God, your sanctification" (1 Thess. 4:3). This means that we are to conform to the image of God, and this we can do only by His grace. We do not have any power to change ourselves; that also must come from Him. Allowing ourselves to be influenced by the world, the flesh and the devil will interrupt the sanctifying process.

We will also interfere with the process when trying to change the world becomes our primary focus. On the other hand, if our goal is to become the person God created us to be, no other person or thing on Earth can prevent that from happening. Not even Satan can stop us.

For example, how should we respond when the government turns a deaf ear to the Church or when other people show contempt for the Lord? Is it our job to take on the government or try to change those who are blasphemous? Those who try will only become angry controllers or very depressed. We are called by God to submit to governing authorities and pray for them (see Rom. 13:1-6; 1 Tim. 2:1-2). We are also to accept one another as Christ has accepted us (see Rom. 15:7). That does not mean we approve of sin or allow others to determine who we are. All Christians must learn how to establish scriptural boundaries to protect themselves from further abuse.

THE CAN-DO SPIRIT

It is a sin to take away another person's courage when they can do all things through Christ who strengthens them (see Phil. 4:13). Anyone who sows the seeds of helplessness and discouragement will reap the harvest of depression. On the other hand, anyone who sows encouragement will reap a rich spiritual harvest.

Christians have been somewhat reluctant to buy into what is called the "power of positive thinking." And some of the arguments against it are good ones. However, we cannot ignore the affect the mind has on our lives. Thinking is a function of the mind and it cannot exceed the mind's inputs and attributes. Any attempt to push the mind beyond its limitations will only result in moving from the world of reality to the world of fantasy.

However, what people can do when they believe in themselves is impressive. Most of humankind live far below their potential. It is estimated that most people use only 5 percent of their brain capacity.

The Sky Is Not the Limit

Some people in the 1950s were saying humankind would never reach the moon. But when Russia launched Sputnik, the United States rose to the challenge. Within a few years, the United States had not only surpassed the Russians, but also Neil Armstrong had actually set foot on the moon. His achievement inspired a lot of confidence in what humans could do if they only believed they could.

About the time the Apollo space program was shutting down, a new program was envisioned. Originally it was called Shuttle Bus. The idea was to create a reentry rocket or capsule that could be used again and again. When the government issued proposals and requested bids from aerospace companies, the technology to build such a craft did not exist. But flushed with the success of the Apollo program, supporters actually believed it could be done, given enough time and money. Today, launching a space shuttle is so commonplace that the public barely notices.

There seems to be no limit to what humans can do. Endowed by the Creator with incredible mental and physical powers, we have launched satellites that make global communication routine. We have learned how to transplant hearts, kidneys, livers and other organs, allowing people to live far longer than ever before. Some people have climbed the highest peaks, descended to the lowest depths of the ocean and probed outer space, going where no man has ever gone before. Others keep adding inches or chopping seconds off world records that were deemed impossible to break decades ago.

Yet There Are Limits

Even with all of the impressive accomplishments, there is a limit to what finite humans can do. We still have not solved the problems of poverty, war, crime or corruption. In spite of all our accomplishments, faith in science as the hope for humanity has actually diminished in this postmodern era.

People, nonetheless, still try to come up with their own answers. Enter the New Age. Out with humanism, in with spiritism. "Of course, people as finite creatures are limited," some people will say. "But what if we are really gods and only need to become aware of our divine nature? There would be no limit to what we could do. We wouldn't need a Savior; we would only need to be enlightened. We could create reality with our own minds. If we believed hard enough, it would become true."

This kind of thinking is nothing more than old-fashioned occultism dressed up in New Age clothing. It seems that when mediums are called channelers and they speak of spirit guides instead of demons, a naive public will buy it! We have come a long way yet returned to the beginning—all the way back to the Garden of Eden, where Satan whispered the ultimate lie: "For God knows that in the day you eat from it *your eyes will be opened, and you will be like God*, knowing good and evil" (Gen. 3:5, emphasis added).

To have knowledge of good and evil implied to Adam and Eve that they could be the origin or determiner of what is good or evil, and what is true or untrue. When they ate the fruit of the forbidden tree, they were in essence saying, "We reject God as the One who determines what is right and wrong. We will determine for ourselves what is good for us and what is true." They played right into the hands of the devil, who is the deceiver and the father of lies.

In a distorted way, Satan was right. Adam and Eve *acted* like gods in determining for themselves what is true and what is right. But what they determined was not right, and rather than embrace the truth that would preserve their lives and freedom, they believed a lie that led to death and bondage to sin.

Today Satan is up to his same old tricks, and they are dangerous because they are built on this half-truth. We are not gods, and we do not create reality with our minds. Believing something does not make it true, no matter how hard we try. God is the ultimate reality. He is the truth, which means that what He says is true. It is for that reason we believe it. Both the humanist and the spiritist are playing god and are creating disastrous results.

The Power of Believing the Truth

We *are* created in the image of God. We are not helpless, because, by the grace of God, we can respond in a responsible way to the reality of this world. We have access to a greater power than human potential: *the power of believing the truth*. If we knew the truth as revealed in God's Word and chose to believe it, the Word would set us free from artificial limitations. We would rarely, if ever, feel discouraged or helpless.

If men can accomplish what they have while exalting themselves as the object of their own faith, imagine what they could accomplish if the object of their faith was God! Jesus said, "With men this is impossible, but with God all things are possible" (Matt. 19:26).

We do not determine what is included in "all things." We cannot decide for ourselves all that we can do or what is true by twisting this verse to say "I believe it, so I can do it." That would be playing god. Every believer has to assume responsibility for being "transformed by the renewing of your mind. Then you will be able to test and approve what God's will is—his good, pleasing and perfect will" (Rom. 12:2, *NIV*).

The real issue is: Do you believe that God's will is good, pleasing and perfect for you? When we were dead in our trespasses and sins, we lacked the presence of God in our lives. In such a state we wanted and needed much more than we had, but we were unable to obtain it on our own. Without the knowledge of God's ways, we developed a "learned helplessness."

Applying "I Can" Thoughts Practically

Paul wrote to the Romans:

Jesus defeated the devil and made us brand-new creations in Himself. He set us free from our pasts. We have to destroy those old strongholds that say "I can't," and replace them with the truth that "we can" in Christ.

And we rejoice in the hope of the glory of God. Not only so, but we also rejoice in our sufferings, because we know that suffering produces perseverance; perseverance, character; and character, hope. And hope does not disappoint us, because God has poured out his love into our hearts by the Holy Spirit, whom he has given us. You see, at just the right time, when we were still powerless, Christ died for the ungodly (Rom. 5:2-6, *NIV*).

Jesus defeated the devil and made us brand-new creations in Himself. He set us free from our pasts. We have to destroy those old strongholds that say "I can't" and replace them with the truth that "we can" in Christ.

The human tendency is to say "This home is hopeless" and then think the solution is to try to change our home by running away. The same holds true for any depressing situation. The answer is neither to try to change the situation nor to let the situation determine who you are. The answer is to work with God in the process of changing yourself.

According to Paul, our hope does not lie in avoiding the trials and tribulations of life, because they are inevitable. Our hope lies in persevering through those trials and becoming more like Christ. The hope that comes from proven character will never disappoint us. Only through proven character will we positively influence the world.

Phil Callaway in his book *Who Put the Skunk in the Trunk?* illustrates this point:

> I'm learning that some of the most successful people I know didn't have a clue what the future held on graduation day.
>
> I'm learning that a good sense of humor is money in the bank. In life. On the job. In a marriage.
>
> I'm learning that a good attitude can control situations you can't. That any bad experience can be a good one. It all depends on me.
>
> I'm learning that you can do something in an instant, that will give you heartache for life.
>
> I'm learning that bitterness and gossip accomplish nothing, but forgiveness and love accomplish everything.
>
> I'm learning that it takes years to build trust, and seconds to destroy it.
>
> I'm learning that if I'm standing on the edge of a cliff, the best way forward is to back up. You don't fail when you lose, you fail when you quit.
>
> I'm learning that too many people spend a lifetime stealing time from those who love them the most, trying to please the ones who care about them the least.
>
> I'm learning that money is a lousy way of keeping score. That true success is not measured in cars, or

homes or bank accounts, but in relationships. Put God first. The others will follow.

I'm learning that having enough money isn't nearly as much fun as I thought it would be when I didn't have any. That money buys less than you think. A house but not a home. Vacations but not peace. Sex but not love.

I'm learning that helping others is far more rewarding than helping myself. That those who laugh more worry less. That when I grow up I wanna be a kid.

I'm learning that you cannot make anyone love you. But you can work on being lovable.

I'm learning that I will never regret a moment spent reading the Bible or praying. Or a kind word. Or a day at the beach.

I'm learning that laughter and tears are nothing to be ashamed of. To celebrate the good things. And pray about the bad.

And I'm learning that the most important thing in the world is loving God. That everything good comes from that.[2]

TWENTY CANS OF SUCCESS

Someone once said that success comes in "cans," and failure comes in "cannots." Here are 20 cans of success you would do well to read for the next 40 days and memorize:

1. Why should I say I can't when the Bible says I can do all things through Christ who gives me strength (Phil. 4:13)?

2. Why should I worry about my needs when I know that God will take care of all my needs according to His riches in glory in Christ Jesus (Phil. 4:19)?

3. Why should I fear when the Bible says God has not given me a spirit of fear but of power, love and a sound mind (2 Tim. 1:7)?

4. Why should I lack faith to live for Christ when God has given me a measure of faith (Rom. 12:3)?

5. Why should I be weak when the Bible says that the Lord is the strength of my life and that I will display strength and take action because I know God (Ps. 27:1; Dan. 11:32)?

6. Why should I allow Satan control over my life when He that is in me is greater than he that is in the world (1 John 4:4)?

7. Why should I accept defeat when the Bible says that God always leads me in victory (2 Cor. 2:14)?

8. Why should I lack wisdom when I know that Christ became wisdom to me from God and that God gives wisdom to me generously when I ask Him for it (1 Cor. 1:30; Jas. 1:5)?

9. Why should I be depressed when I can recall to mind God's lovingkindness, compassion and faithfulness, and have hope (Lam. 3:21-23)?

10. Why should I worry and be upset when I can cast all my anxieties on Christ, who cares for me (1 Pet. 5:7)?

11. Why should I ever be in bondage when I know that there is freedom where the Spirit of the Lord is (Gal. 5:1)?

12. Why should I feel condemned when the Bible says there is no condemnation for those who are in Christ Jesus (Rom. 8:1)?

13. Why should I feel alone when Jesus said He is with me always and will never leave me nor forsake me (Matt. 28:20; Heb. 13:5)?

14. Why should I feel like I'm cursed or have bad luck when the Bible says that Christ rescued me from the curse of

the law that I might receive His Spirit by faith (Gal. 3:13-14)?

15. Why should I be unhappy when I, like Paul, can learn to be content whatever the circumstances (Phil. 4:11)?

16. Why should I feel worthless when Christ became sin for me so that I might become the righteousness of God (2 Cor. 5:21)?

17. Why should I feel helpless in the presence of others when I know that if God is for me, who can be against me (Rom. 8:31)?

18. Why should I be confused when God is the author of peace and He gives me knowledge through His Spirit, who lives in me (1 Cor. 2:12; 14:33)?

19. Why should I feel like a failure when I am more than a conqueror through Christ who loved me (Rom. 8:37)?

20. Why should I let the pressures of life bother me when I can take courage knowing that Jesus has overcome the world and its problems (John 16:33)?[3]

DEPRESSION BUSTERS

Read:

1 Samuel 17

Reflect:

1. Although the Bible says we can do all things through Christ who strengthens us (see Phil. 4:13), why are we sometimes overwhelmed by the belief that we are unable to affect our world for Christ?
2. What is learned helplessness and how did it affect the children of Israel?
3. How have you personally been affected by learned helplessness? How can we overcome it?
4. How is biblical trust, or faith, different from the *power of positive thinking*?
5. What are some of the dangers of the New Age *power of positive thinking* system?

Respond:

Dear Lord, why should I say I can't when the Bible says I can do all things through Christ who gives me strength (see Phil. 4:13)? Lord, I know that I have been conditioned by the world and developed many patterns of hopeless thinking. I turn from this hopelessness now and turn to You, the God of hope, and choose now to believe that I can in fact do all the things You have for me to do. I know that without You I can do nothing, but with You, Lord, all things that are in line with You and Your will are possible for me. In Jesus' name I pray. Amen.

Notes

1. Alice Gray, comp., *Stories for the Extreme Teen's Heart* (Sisters, OR: Multnomah Publishers, 2000), pp. 164-165.
2. Phil Callaway, *Who Put a Skunk in the Trunk?* (Sisters, OR: Multnomah Publishers, 1999), n.p.
3. Neil T. Anderson and Dave Park, *Stomping Out the Darkness* (Ventura, CA: Regal Books, 1993), pp. 103-104.

CHAPTER 10

SURVIVING THE DARKNESS—DEALING WITH LOSS

Weeping may last for the night, but a shout of joy comes in the morning

PSALM 30:5

He is no fool who gives up what he cannot keep to gain what he cannot lose.

JIM ELLIOT, JOURNAL ENTRY, OCTOBER 28, 1949

Fourteen-year-old Greg and fifteen-year-olds Jonathan and Todd squeezed into the back seat of the tiny compact car. Marcus climbed into the front seat, and Matt who had obtained his driver's license two weeks earlier, slid behind the steering wheel. The quintet of classmates and teammates headed to a surprise birthday party for a friend. Matt steered the car out of the little town where they all lived and onto the county road heading west. The road soon turned northwest, and the car topped sixty-five miles per hour. Suddenly the right tire went off the side of the road onto the uneven shoulder; Matt swung the steering wheel sharply to the left. The car immediately went into a slide that carried it across the road, where it slammed into a utility pole and rolled over on its top, crumpling the roof.

At some point, the boys in the front were thrown free of the car and received relatively minor injuries; Jonathan, Todd and Greg, who were pushed tightly against the rear of the car as it spun off the road, were crushed as the roof crumpled beneath the weight of the car. All three died before help arrived.

The school and community reeled from the news. The three victims, all A or B students, were well liked. Their families were highly involved in school and community events. Their friends, classmates, teachers and coaches sobbed in each other's arms in the school hallways on the Monday morning following the accident. Some walked the halls in a daze. Others became physically sick.

The school administration arranged for counselors to be present all day Monday and Tuesday, and students were not required to go to classes; they were permitted to linger in the cafeteria, talking to counselors and friends, for as long as they needed. The school's compassionate response was appreciated by the friends and family of the boys, but the grief felt by so many was nonetheless overwhelming.

"We're a very tight-knit community," the high school principal told the local newspaper, "and it's going to take us all a very long time to completely heal."[1]

THE RESPONSE OF SADNESS

The melancholy at the school that followed the loss of the three boys is called *reactive depression*. This emotional response to any crisis of life is the most common form of depression. But the crisis itself does not cause the depression. Our mental perception of external events, based on what we believe and the way our minds have been programmed, is what determines how we feel and react.

People typically go through a very predictable cycle when they experience a crisis, as depicted in the following diagram:

CRISIS REACTION CYCLE

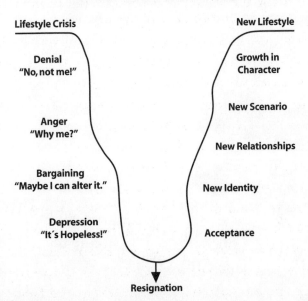

Lifestyle Crisis

Denial
"No, not me!"

Anger
"Why me?"

Bargaining
"Maybe I can alter it."

Depression
"It's Hopeless!"

Resignation

New Lifestyle

Growth in Character

New Scenario

New Relationships

New Identity

Acceptance

Most of us settle into a lifestyle we assume will continue indefinitely or will, hopefully, improve. We make plans for the weekend and summer vacations, counting on life to go on as scheduled. We schedule daily events with the hope that we will still be alive, our health will be fine and all of the conditions necessary for life to go on as it has will be favorable.

Some people take a fatalistic approach to tomorrow. They say with Solomon, when he limited his view to things under the sun, "That which has been is that which will be. . . . So, there is nothing new under the sun" (Eccles. 1:9). Such people make no realistic plans, and consequently they end up having no meaningful future.

Others, even Christians, presume upon the future. James has some sobering advice for anyone who does that:

> Now listen, you who say, "Today or tomorrow we will go to this or that city, spend a year there, carry on business and make money." Why, you do not even know what will happen tomorrow. What is your life? You are a mist that appears for a little while and then vanishes. Instead, you ought to say, "If it is the Lord's will, we will live and do this or that." As it is, you boast and brag. All such boast-

The will of God will not take us where the grace of God cannot keep us.

ing is evil. Anyone, then, who knows the good he ought to do and doesn't do it, sins (Jas. 4:13-17, *NIV*).

The good, which we ought to do, is the Lord's will; therefore, we must choose to live responsible lives, one day at a time. The will of God will not take us where the grace of God cannot keep us.

In the Sermon on the Mount, Jesus tells us not to worry about tomorrow. If God takes care of the lilies of the fields and the birds of the air, will He not much more provide for us? (see Matt. 6:26-30). Because our heavenly Father knows our needs, we must "seek first His kingdom and his righteousness; and all these things shall be added to [us]. Therefore do not be anxious for tomorrow; for tomorrow will care for itself. Each day has enough trouble of its own" (Matt. 6:33-34).

This does not mean that we should make no plans for tomorrow. We have to have some foresight to live responsibly. However, the primary purpose for setting goals and making plans for the future is to give us meaningful direction for our lives today. Because we do not have control over many circumstances that can totally disrupt those plans, we need to say, "Lord willing, tomorrow we will do [fill in the blank], and regardless of what tomorrow holds, we will trust Him." This requires us to mentally and emotionally prepare for impermanence.

BE PREPARED FOR CHANGE

In five years, nothing will be as it is now. There is no permanence—there is only change. The Lord tried to prepare His disciples for this reality when He told them three times "that the Son of Man must suffer many things and be rejected by the elders and the chief priests and the scribes, be killed, and after three days rise again. And He was stating the matter plainly" (Mark 8:31-32).

The disciples' first response was denial. Peter actually rebuked the Lord (see Mark 8:32). When He told them a second time what was going to happen to Him, they did not understand what He meant and were afraid to ask (see Mark 9:32). They did not want to talk about it.

Finally, as Jesus and His fearful disciples approached Jerusalem, He told them a third time what was going to happen (see Mark 10:32-34). His purpose for telling them in advance was to teach them the principle that the Messiah must die to purchase salvation for humankind and to give them hope when they faced persecution. He wanted to assure them that even though He would be killed, He would rise again.

Hope does not lie in the possibility of permanence or in avoiding trials and tribulations. Hope lies in the proven character that comes from persevering through them. Neither does our hope lie in the eternal preservation of our physical bodies. Our hope lies in the Resurrection.

To survive the crises of life, we must have an eternal perspective. Without such a perspective, we cannot see the hope of summer during the emotional winters of our soul. The "deceptive present" masks the possibility of any hope for tomorrow. The psalmist's statement "Precious in the sight of the LORD is the death of His godly ones" (Ps. 116:15) does not make sense from a time-bound perspective. But it makes complete sense from an eternal perspective.

STAGES OF GRIEF

Grief and reactive depression can arise from any crisis that interferes with our plans. It could be the loss of a job, a health problem (our own or a loved one's) or the end of our dreams. Such losses sow the seeds of depression when we fail to see that our times are in His hands. Let us take a look at the first three stages of grief as diagrammed in the preceding chart—the phases teenagers often go through on the way to the depths of depression.

Denial: No, Not Me!

The first response is often denial, a refusal to accept the crisis or the loss. Some people may find it too painful to face the truth. They consciously or subconsciously think, *This is all a bad dream or a trick that someone is playing on me. I refuse to even consider this as real.* Or they may consciously choose to not entertain thoughts that this crisis or loss actually happened. *I'll deal with this tomorrow or maybe next month.* Some people may make many attempts to recover what has been lost or go on living as though the loss never happened.

Anger: Why Me?

Denial can last for 30 seconds or 30 years. When people finally face the truth, they feel angry or resentful, because what happened to them was not fair. They think, *Why is this happening to me?* Their anger can be directed toward others, including God, whom they think caused the crisis. Those who feel guilty or ashamed direct their anger toward themselves.

Bargaining: Maybe I Can Change It

After the anger has simmered, some people start to bargain. They reason, *Maybe I can change the situation or undo the events that led up to this crisis.* They become depressed when they discover they cannot do anything to change what has happened nor can they reverse the consequences. They then believe the situation is hopeless and that they are helpless to do anything about it. They tried to undo it all but could not. Now they are not sure if they can go on living with the present circumstances. The tragic loss seems too much to bear. It is the winter of the soul. How can a person in these circumstances even possibly imagine what summer is like again?

A Time to Mourn

It is natural, normal and certainly not sinful to mourn the loss of anything that is morally good or even morally neutral. However, inordinate, destructive or inappropriate grief can lead to serious depression. It is normal to grieve the loss of a loved one, but note how Paul would help us guard against destructive grief over a loved one who has died in the Lord:

> But we do not want you to be uninformed, brethren, about those who are asleep, that you may not grieve, as do the rest who have no hope. For if we believe that Jesus died and rose again, even so God will bring with Him those who have fallen asleep in Jesus (1 Thess. 4:13-14).

We are protected from destructive grief when our hope lies in the finished work of Christ, not in the things of this world that we have no right or ability to control. We grieve for that which we have lost because we have become attached to certain people, places, ideas and things. The extent of the grief is determined by the degree of attachment we had, whether appropriate or not.

In Losing, We Win

Paul was deeply attached to the Pharisaic traditions and customs of his people, and he had worked hard to achieve his status and place in life. For him to give all that up would require a massive intervention by God.

It came suddenly on the road to Damascus. Paul was struck down and blinded by the power of God. All his hopes for a successful future were dashed in a moment. "Why, God?" he must have asked. "Why did You do this to me? Nobody has been more zealous for You than I." To make matters worse, his only hope would come from the Church he had so fervently persecuted. Reflecting on this later in life, Paul wrote:

> But whatever things were gain to me, those things I have counted as loss for the sake of Christ. More than that, I count all things to be loss in view of the surpassing value of knowing Christ Jesus my Lord, for whom I suffered the loss of all things, and count them but rubbish in order that I may gain Christ (Phil. 3:7-8).

Missionary Jim Elliot wrote in his diary, "He is no fool who gives up what he cannot keep to gain what he cannot lose."[2] There is nothing on Earth that we cannot lose. This is the central teaching of all four Gospels. "For whoever wishes to save his life shall lose it; but whoever loses his life for My sake shall find it. For what will a man be profited, if he gains the whole world, and forfeits his soul?" (Matt. 16:25-26).

The first reference to life in this passage refers to the soul, which is life that comes from humans. The second reference to life refers to the spirit, which is life that comes from God. He who finds his life within himself will eventually lose it. He who finds his life in God will keep it for all eternity.

In other words, those who find their identity, security and sense of worth in the natural order of things will lose them. We cannot take them with us. Whatever name we made for ourselves, whatever fame we achieved, whatever earthly position we attained and whatever treasures we were able to amass—all will be left behind. Attachments to this world subtract from our attachment to Christ.

On the other hand, nothing can separate us from the love of God, and we will suffer no debilitating loss that we cannot endure if we find our life, identity, acceptance, security and significance in Christ.

Destructive, reactive depression signifies an overattachment to people, places, ideas and things that we have no right or ability to control. It indicates that we simply will not let go of something we are going to lose anyway or have already lost.

In Africa, monkeys are caught using a hollowed-out coconut shell that has a chained attached to it. The other end of the chain is tied to a tree or a stake in the ground. Then the hunters put some favorite monkey food in the hollowed-out shell. The monkey comes along and puts his fist into the shell to get the food. But when he makes a fist around the food, he can no longer take out his hand from the shell. Then the hunters simply detach the chain from the tree or stake and walk off with the monkey.

Why doesn't the monkey just let go? Who knows? Why don't we?

EXPLANATORY STYLES

Difficult times will set up roadblocks on the path to wholeness and maturity. Some people bounce back quickly, but others struggle for weeks or months, and some never recover. Most people learn how to accept and grow through all kinds of childhood mistakes, adolescent embarrassments, young-adult misunderstandings and adult problems. Some have had more than their share of bad times. God must have known that they had broad shoulders—or perhaps He was preparing them for a special ministry of helping others through their own crises.

Why do some people recover faster than others who face the same crisis? Does one have greater health or greater support from others? The major difference in our ability to recover is found in the way we perceive events that befall us. Our beliefs about these events, ourselves and God will determine if we respond in fear, despair or faith.

We interpret trials and tribulations through the grid of our previous learning experiences. We attempt to explain what happened and why it happened. How we explain difficult circumstances and painful events is drawn from our beliefs about God, ourselves and others and the way we think the world works.

Permanence: It Will Last Forever

The speed of our recovery is greatly affected by whether we think the consequences of the crisis will have a short-term or a long-term effect on us. If we think our problems today will negatively affect us all our lives, then we will become pessimistic, believe that the situation is hopeless and consequently feel depressed.

This kind of thinking is so commonplace that we are hardly aware of it. Suppose a student thinks, *My dad is cranky. He must be in a bad mood.* That is a short-term problem, and it will have very little lasting effect upon the student. The student may decide to avoid confrontation until the mood passes. But if the student thinks, *My dad is cranky. He is an irritable person*, the student is viewing the situation as a long-term problem. His response could vary:

- "I'm going to ignore him." That is denial.
- "I'm going to try controlling him." That is anger.
- "I'm going to try appeasing him." That is bargaining.
- "I'm going to try to change him." That will be depressing!
- "I'm going to avoid him." That is resignation.

- "I'm going to love him and learn to live with him." That is acceptance.
- "I cannot change what has happened, but by the grace of God I can change. I can come through this crisis a better person." That is growth.

There are many crisis events and losses that cannot be altered, and that will result in our having to live with the consequences all our lives. Difficult circumstances are opportunities to adjust our course of life. When a pilot encounters turbulent air while flying, he may consider going higher or lower, but stopping is a poor option. Someone once said, "A bend in the road is not the end of the road unless you fail to make the turn."

Joni Eareckson Tada must have felt that her life had come to the end of the road when as a young woman she found herself paralyzed after a swimming accident. In an interview recorded in June 1993 for a Focus on the Family program, she said, "I wanted to end my life, and the frustration I felt at not being able to do that only intensified my depression. I was so desperate, I begged one of my friends to help me end it all." Thank God that she could not, and thank God that He enabled Joni to make the bend in the road and become a blessing to millions through her ministry, Joni and Friends.

The Lord said, "For I know the plans that I have for you . . . plans for welfare and not for calamity to give you a future and a hope" (Jer. 29:11).

When we are in the darkness of depression, it is easy to believe the lie that God's favor is only momentary and His anger will last forever. But the truth is, "His anger is but for a moment, His favor is for a lifetime; weeping may last for the night, but a shout of joy comes in the morning" (Ps. 30:5).

Winter is not permanent. Even if we cannot sense the warmth of summer, we must choose to believe that summer will come.

When we think our crisis is permanent, then we can consider again the words of Jeremiah in Lamentations 3:19-23 (*NIV*):

> I remember my affliction and my wandering, the bitterness and the gall. I well remember them, and my soul is downcast within me. Yet this I call to mind and therefore I have hope: because of the LORD's great love we are not consumed, for his compassions never fail. They are new every morning; great is your faithfulness.

Pervasiveness: It Will Ruin My Whole Life

The grid of pervasiveness refers to the extent to which a crisis can affect other areas of our lives. For example, this happens when we think that because we failed in one endeavor, we must be a total failure, or when we think that our lives are over because we were turned down or rejected by someone on whom we based our future.

Remember Jan's story in chapter 1? She went through a painful breakup with her boyfriend. She mourned the loss of a loved one with whom she hoped to spend the rest of her life. *Would anyone ever want to marry me?* she wondered.

"His compassions never fail. They are new every morning; great is your faithfulness."

Jan cried incessantly for the first two and a half days—and on and off after that. She did not want to be around anybody, and she began skipping school. Jan's explanatory style led her to think that her family and friends would eventually discover her to be inadequate, so why should she bother trying? Her friends called, but she often did not return their calls. When she did, she was cold and distant. The loss in one area of her life was projected onto every other area. Consequently, she felt there was no hope.

Do not let one loss take over other aspects of your life. If you experience loss, it does not mean you are a loser in life. If you fail to accomplish one goal, you are not a failure. If you get laid off at work, it does not necessarily mean you are irresponsible.

The tendency of this kind of thinking is to rest our whole sense of worth on one relationship, experience, idea or plan. When plans or relationships do not last or fail to materialize, we wrongly tag ourselves failures.

Personalization: It's Me! It's All My Fault!

In personalization, the depressed person feels responsible for another person's anger, for the downsizing of a corporation, for bad weather, for not knowing the future and for a host of other uncontrollable circumstances and situations.

Many teens become depressed and think it is their fault when their parents get divorced. Many perfectionists struggle with depression, because they have a tendency to blame themselves for everything that goes wrong. One little crisis upsets their idealized world and they think, *It's my fault*. They become so driven to achieve their self-made goals that they become supersensitive to any failure or crisis.

Personalization distorts a person's perception of reality. When a crisis erupts, some people immediately think, *What did I do now?* They may go to their room and obsessively review the incident, looking for what they did wrong. They live on "if onlys":

"If only I had done that, she would never have left me" or "If only I had studied more when I had a chance, I would have gotten a better grade."

Much of the identity of such people rides on the successful outcome of life's pivotal events. That is backward thinking. Their identity and their future rests on identifying who they are in Christ and the truth that there is now no condemnation for those who are in Him (see Rom. 8:1).

Many of these people were wrongly accused in early childhood, and they have come to believe they have a part to play in every negative thing that happens. Paul says, "Let no one keep defrauding you of your prize by delighting in self-abasement" (Col. 2:18).

Others are just victims of the accuser, Satan, who accuses them day and night. They have never understood the battle for their minds, nor learned how to take every thought captive to the obedience of Christ.

Blaming ourselves for every crisis in life and for every slight imperfection is a sure way to open the door to a failure identity and to depression. On the other hand, blaming others is a sure way to become bitter, angry, proud, self-serving and abusive. Self-exaltation is as bad as self-condemnation. "For through the grace given to me I say to every man among you not to think more highly of himself than he ought to think; but to think so as to have sound judgment, as God has allotted to each a measure of faith" (Rom 12:3). It does not do any good to blame others, and it does not do any good to blame ourselves. Neither pride nor false humility is a proper response to the trials and tribulations of life.

GETTING OUT OF THE RUT

- It's my fault that our football team didn't win all of its games (personalization).

- Now I'll never get the scholarship I wanted (permanence).
- I'm a total failure in life (pervasiveness)!

The elements of personalization, permanence and pervasiveness dominate the way depressed people think. How can we change these grids that distort our perception of reality?

If we experience loss in one area, we must avoid expanding that into a total life crisis. We must keep it specific. If we experience a crisis today, we cannot allow it to affect us tomorrow. We must keep short accounts. If the world is disintegrating around us, we cannot accept the blame unless we really did make the mistake that caused it all.

If we suffer the consequences of a bad decision, then we must change what we can, cut our losses and move on. If we have committed a willful act of sin, then we must own up to it. "If we confess our sins, He is faithful and righteous to forgive us our sins and to cleanse us from all unrighteousness" (1 John 1:9).

Depression is an intertwining of the body, soul and spirit, all of which are regulated by what we believe. Jesus said, "You shall know the truth, and the truth shall make you free" (John 8:32). Choosing to believe the truth and living by faith must be in place for us to live an emotionally healthy and productive life.

The converse is also true. Believing a lie and thinking unwholesome thoughts will fuel depression and lead to bondage. You can change what you believe and how you think— and this change must happen if you are going to be free from depression.

Changing Wrong Beliefs

The story is told of a frog who was hopping around a pasture. It had rained the day before, and the soil was very damp. A truck had driven through the pasture and cut deep ruts in the ground. Unintentionally, the frog bounced into one of those ruts and got stuck. He made a halfhearted attempt to hop out but did not make it. The rut was too deep.

The next day a few of the frog's friends came looking for him, and they found him stuck in a rut. They encouraged him to try again to jump out, but the frog said it was hopeless. He was permanently stuck in a rut and was no longer good for anything. The frog further thought, *It was probably my fault that it rained the other day. That was just God's way of getting even with me for not being a better frog.* For five straight days the other frogs came by to encourage the stuck frog, but he remained in the rut.

On the sixth day, the frog's friends were surprised to see the frog hopping around the field. They ask how he managed to get unstuck. "Oh," he said, "a big truck came along and I *had* to get out of there!"

Fortunately, we do not have to stay in the rut of accepting fatalistically any of the three preceding explanatory styles. We can change these grids:

From:	To:
Personal: "I'm the problem"	Impersonal: "It's a problem"
Permanent: "Forever"	Temporary: "For a season"
Pervasive: "In everything"	Specific: "In this one thing"

How do we get unstuck? The first step is to define the crisis and then put it into perspective. We can never change if we deny the crisis.

Is the Loss Real or Imaginary?

Analyzing the crisis helps to determine if the perceived loss is real or only imagined. Many young people have gone all the way to the bottom of the crisis cycle only to find out that what they had believed or heard was not true. This can easily happen in the early stages of diagnosing a physical illness. One lady was so sure that her husband was going to die from cancer that before the doctor ever gave a diagnosis, she was bargaining with God to save his life. It turned out that her husband did not have cancer at all.

It is possible to go through all the stages of anger, bargaining and depression when the crisis is only a feared or potential loss.

We can choose to mentally dwell upon facts or assumptions. The soul does not need facts to begin to worry. And that worry easily turns into fear and fear turns into despair. The emotional result is the same whether the crisis is real or imagined.

Every real loss that is acknowledged will result in some degree of mourning. Denying the loss only robs us of the comfort we need. Jesus said, "Blessed are those who mourn, for they shall be comforted" (Matt. 5:4). Christians are real people who bleed when they are cut and cry when they are hurt. It takes time to adjust to a loss.

Beware of Excessive Attachment

Excessive grief about any loss can turn into depression. It may indicate that too much value was placed on one or more attachments. This requires an honest evaluation of the loss in light of eternity, and a decision to let go of the past and grab hold of God. Paul tells us:

> Not that I have already obtained all this, or have already been made perfect, but I press on to take hold of that for which Christ Jesus took hold of me. Brothers, I do not consider myself yet to have taken hold of it. But one thing I do: Forgetting what is behind and straining toward what is ahead, I press on toward the goal to win the prize for which God has called me heavenward in Christ Jesus. All of us who are mature should take such a view of things. And if on some point you think differently, that too God will make clear to you. Only let us live

up to what we have already attained (Phil. 3:12-16, *NIV*).

Avoid Blame and Guilt

Casting blame or feeling guilty are inappropriate responses to loss and will only prolong the grieving period. We must accept the cards that have been dealt to us, realizing that God "causes His sun to rise on the evil and the good, and sends rain on the righteous and the unrighteous" (Matt. 5:45).

Evaluate What You Have and Who You Are

We are all in the same boat. None of us will make the journey through life without facing many trials and tribulations. Even if we lived a perfect life, we would still experience considerable loss. Therefore, we should never forget: What we have to gain in Christ is far greater than any loss we will be called to endure. We do not bargain with God. We humbly submit to Him. And we pray the serenity prayer:

> *God, grant me the serenity*
> *To accept the things I cannot change,*
> *The courage to change the things I can,*
> *And the wisdom to know the difference.*

Recovery from any crisis is going to call for a deeper evaluation of who we really are. We may have placed too much of our identity in the things we do and not enough in who we are in Christ.

Crises not only help us clarify who we are and why we are here, but they also create the need for new relationships and the need to construct a new, godly plan for our lives. These changes were probably necessary for our growth in the Lord, but we would never have made those changes if we had not been forced to do so.

Buzz Aldrin, the second man to walk on the moon, said, "My depression forced me, at the age of 41, to stop and, for the first time, examine my life."[3] We can easily get stuck in the same old ruts until God brings a truck along and we have to move. Read the words of Hebrews 12:7-11 (*NIV*):

> Endure hardship as discipline; God is treating you as sons. For what son is not disciplined by his father? If you are not disciplined (and everyone undergoes discipline), then you are illegitimate children and not true sons. Moreover, we have all had human fathers who disciplined us and we respected them for it. How much more should we submit to the Father of our spirits and live! Our fathers disciplined us for a little while as they thought best; but God disciplines us for our good, that we may share in his holiness. No discipline seems pleasant at the time, but painful. Later on, however, it produces a harvest of righteousness and peace for those who have been trained by it.

God wants us to share in His holiness. The purpose of His discipline is to produce godly character. In addition, we will all be victimized as the inevitable consequence of living in a fallen world. Whether we remain victims is our choice. We have the potential to come through every crisis and become a better person. When we do, our resultant lifestyle will be higher and more godly.

Therefore, in the winter of your discouragement, lift up your eyes to heaven. Recall that your hope is in God and that you will again experience the warmth of summer and the harvest of fall.

DEPRESSION BUSTERS

Read:

Philippians 3:12-16

Reflect:

1. What is the most common form of depression that young people face?
2. List the typical crisis reaction cycle that we talked about in this chapter.
3. What are the three explanatory styles that we talked about in this chapter?
4. Have you experienced a loss or losses in your life? If so, what explanatory styles did you experience in your life? Were you able to get out of the rut?

Respond:

Dear Lord, I confess that at times I have not always forgotten my dark past, what is behind, and strained toward what is ahead—a new life in Christ. Lord, I want to grab on to my future and not my past. I want to trust in Christ and not my bad track record. I choose now to press on toward the goal to win the prize for which God has called me heavenward in Christ Jesus. I want to walk in freedom and not depression. In Jesus' name I pray. Amen.

Notes

1. Josh McDowell and Bob Hostetler, *Handbook on Counseling Youth* (Dallas, TX: Word Publishing, 1996), p. 92.
2. Jim Elliot, "Jim Elliot Quote," from Elliot's journal, October 28, 1949, *Billy Graham Center Archives*, May 17, 2001. http://www.wheaton.edu/bgc/archives/faq/20.htm (accessed August 1, 2001).
3. Buzz Aldrin, "Return To Earth," quoted in *Current Biographic Yearbook*, 1993.

CHAPTER 11

CLIMBING TO THE TOP–SUFFERING FOR RIGHTEOUSNESS

Beloved, do not be surprised at the fiery ordeal among you, which comes upon you for your testing, as though some strange thing were happening to you; but to the degree that you share the sufferings of Christ, keep on rejoicing; so that also at the revelation of His glory, you may rejoice with exultation. If you are reviled for the name of Christ, you are blessed, because the Spirit of glory and of God rests upon you.

1 PETER 4:12-14

God whispers to us in our pleasures, speaks in our conscience, but shouts in our pains.

C. S. LEWIS, *THE PROBLEM OF PAIN*

We live in a fallen world, and life on this planet is not always fair. We want things to go our way, but they often do not. We want justice to prevail, but that will not always happen in this lifetime. God will make all things right in the end, but until then we will have to live with many injustices. Many Christians struggle with depression because they have never understood the role that suffering has in our sanctification and the fact that suffering is an inevitable consequence of living in a fallen world. We are tempted to think that Christians should not have to suffer if we live a righteous life. Early Christians, however, suffered greatly at the hands of the religious establishment. One account of suffering for Christ is told about 40 athletes who gave up everything to follow Christ:

> During his reign as emperor of Rome, Nero had powerful young wrestlers who competed on his behalf. Every day during their long, arduous workouts and before each tournament, they would chant in unison, "We wrestle for thee alone, O Nero, to win for thee the crown." Among these mighty athletes was Vespasian—a brilliant leader—outstanding in strength and loyalty.
>
> One winter a message was sent to Nero advising him that forty of his wrestlers had become Christians, and they no longer dedicated their power and strength to Nero, but instead to Christ. Nero summoned Vespasian and told him that all forty of the wrestlers were to be killed if they did not renounce their loyalty to Christ. However, rather than kill them outright, the wrestlers were stripped naked and sent out in the bitter cold to spend the night on a frozen lake until they froze to death or renounced their faith.
>
> A group of Roman soldiers built a campfire close to the shore and huddled around the warmth as they

guarded the freezing wrestlers. Vespasian joined the soldiers in their vigil. Throughout a frigid night, the wrestlers called out in unison: "We forty wrestlers for Thee alone, O Christ, to win for Thee the crown." During the darkest hours when the temperature dropped the lowest, their voices became weaker and weaker but still they called out "We forty wrestlers for Thee alone, O Christ, to win for Thee the crown."

Shortly before dawn, one wrestler lost courage and stumbled toward the soldiers and the warmth of the fire. Rather than freeze to death, he would relent. At the edge of the lake you could still hear the faint voices of the other wrestlers, "We thirty-nine wrestlers for Thee alone, O Christ . . ."

As Vespasian heard their pledge, he stripped himself and walked out on the frozen lake to where the others stood. As they rose, the soldiers heard Vespasian's strong voice mingled with the others, "We forty wrestlers for Thee alone, O Christ."[1]

In Early Church times, suffering was something every believer knew was coming his way. Acts 5:41 records this about some of the early followers of Jesus, after they were beaten for sharing what they believed: "They went on their way from the presence of the Council, rejoicing that they had been considered worthy to suffer shame for His name." "Indeed, all who desire to live godly in Christ Jesus will be persecuted" (2 Tim. 3:12).

Persecution is not limited to the past. More Christians were martyred for their faith in 1997 than in any other year in Church history.

Scripture uses many terms to describe suffering, including "affliction," "anguish," "distress," "grief," "misery," "pain," "tribulation" and "chastisement." In addition, various metaphors depict suffering, such as refining fire (see Isa. 48:10; 1 Pet. 1:6-7), overflowing waters (see Isa. 43:2) and birth pangs (see John 16:20-22; Rom. 8:18-22).

Although most of us would rather not face the facts, suffering and anguish are a part of the process of conforming to the image of God. Many Christian teens are depressed because they believe they should not have to suffer. However, suffering plays a critical role in our sanctification. To understand more about sanctification check, out our books *Sold Out* and *Higher Ground* or the devotionals *Real Life* and *Righteous Pursuit*.

WHY WE SUFFER

Why do Christians have to suffer for the sake of righteousness? This next story compares a worldview of suffering with a heavenly perspective and can help us see how God uses suffering.

A loving mother once saved her little girl from a burning house, but suffered severe burns on her hands and arms. When the girl grew up, not knowing how her mother's arms became so seared, she was ashamed of the scarred, gnarled hands and always insisted that her mother wear long gloves to cover up that ugliness.

But one day the daughter asked her mother how her hands became so scarred. For the first time the mother told her the story of how she had saved her life with those hands. The daughter wept tears of gratitude and said, "Oh Mother, those are beautiful hands, the most beautiful in the world. Don't ever hide them again."[2]

The blood of Christ may seem to be a grim and repulsive subject to people who do not realize its true significance, but to those who have accepted His redemption and have been set free from slavery of sin, the blood of Christ is precious. "He is so rich in kindness that he purchased our freedom through the blood of his Son, and our sins are forgiven" (Eph. 1:7, *NLT*).

That girl will never question her mother's love for her, and we never have to question Jesus' love for us. Christ's suffering and sacrifice on the cross demonstrate just how much He loves us. Suffering at times produces terrible scars, but sometimes nothing can better communicate love. We will share in the glory of Christ only if we "share in his sufferings" (Rom. 8:17, *NIV*). "If we endure, we shall also reign with Him" (2 Tim. 2:12). "For just as the sufferings of Christ are ours in abundance, so also our comfort is abundant through Christ" (2 Cor. 1:5).

Much of the suffering believer's experience is related to living for Christ in a hostile world. Trials are destined to come "in spreading the gospel of Christ" (1 Thess. 3:2, *NIV*). The Word further declares, "We must go through many hardships to enter the kingdom of God" (Acts 14:22, *NIV*).

Suffering will also come as the consequence of our own sin and as correction from our heavenly Father. David felt the heavy hand of God in the form of physical and mental suffering as a result of his sin (see Ps. 32:3-5). Even apart from sin, our heavenly Father will discipline us so that we can share in His holiness.

> All discipline for the moment seems not to be joyful, but sorrowful; yet to those who have been trained by it, afterwards it yields the peaceful fruit of righteousness (Heb. 12:11).

Finally, suffering comes simply from our human frailty—we are part of a fallen world. The decaying of the outer man and the accompanying afflictions are part of our normal existence in the present life which is "subject to a thousand troubles and under sentence of death."

THE VALUE OF SUFFERING

Physical pain is a necessary warning signal. Even a lack of proper bodily nourishment causes pain. Suffering in the Christian life can be a sign of sickness, warning us that further problems are coming unless something is changed. Suffering may be God's way of trying to motivate us to change.

Sometimes it takes great suffering to get our attention. As someone has said, "Small trials often make us beside ourselves, but great trials bring us again back to ourselves." Such was the case of the prodigal son. It was only after his food ran out and he said, "I am dying here with hunger" that he "came to his senses," repented and returned to his father (see Luke 15:17-20).

Suffering Builds Character

The trials of life do not break us—they only reveal who we are. The fact that suffering can build character is very clear in the Bible.

Our earthly fathers discipline us for a little while, as they think best. However, God disciplines us for our own good, that we may share in His holiness. No discipline seems pleasant at the time it is given—just painful. Later, however, it produces a harvest of righteousness and peace for those who have been trained by it (see Heb. 12:10-11).

Suffering Draws Us to God

Our love of God is often tainted with our love of the good things He gives us. Suffering strips away any pretense from our relationship with God. It weans us from all that is not of God, that we might learn to love Him for *who* He is, rather than for *what* He gives. Augustine said, "God wants to give us something, but cannot, because our hands are full—there's nowhere for Him to put it." Suffering empties our hands so that God can give us Himself, the true treasure of life.

Through Suffering We Understand God and His Work

We live in a world of conflict. Biblical history reveals a battle between good and evil that has brought much suffering. Even God shares in this suffering because of what sin has done to His creation. As the prophet reveals, God also suffers in the suffering of His people: "In all their affliction He was afflicted" (Isa. 63:9). This reality of evil and the true nature of God's love for us would not be known except through the experience of suffering.

Our suffering in depression can be an opportunity to tell other people about God's sustaining grace and thus be used to draw them to God. Doctors and nurses are far more impressed with godly patients who hold up well under suffering and face death without fear, than with begging, pleading Christians who have no sense of their immortality.

No matter what the source of our suffering, whether directly from God's discipline, from the hand of another person or

In His infinite wisdom and love He allows suffering to come our way for His ultimate glory.

simply from the evil that is part of the fallen world, it is all under the control of God. In His infinite wisdom and love He allows suffering to come our way for His ultimate glory, our growth in character and our witness in this world.

ONLY WHAT YOU CAN BEAR

All of God's reasons for our sufferings may never be fully known in our lifetime. But we can be assured that God always limits the suffering He allows for each of us. Just as He clearly set limits on the suffering Satan could bring on Job, so He does for each of us. Some, such as Job and Paul, obviously had broader shoulders upon which God allowed more suffering to rest for righteousness' sake.

With suffering always comes the temptation to respond with the sin of unbelief, either in despondency that says "God has forsaken me and there is no hope" or in the anger of rebellion that says "I hate you, God, for letting this happen, so forget You. I'm going to go my own way from now on." Satan has scored another victory when the victim believes such lies and walks away from his only source of hope.

Our heavenly Father assures us He will not allow any suffering that we cannot bear:

No temptation [testing or trial] has seized you except what is common to man. And God is faithful; he will not let you be tempted beyond what you can bear [or beyond your strength]. But when you are tempted, he will also provide a way out so that you can [or have the strength to] stand up under it (1 Cor. 10:13, *NIV*).

This promise affirms that God places a limit on our suffering. He knows our strengths and weaknesses in every area of our

The will of God will never take us where the grace of God will not sustain us.

lives—physically, emotionally and spiritually. He will not allow any suffering on any occasion that we cannot handle with His grace. The will of God will never take us where the grace of God will not sustain us.

GOD'S PROVISIONS IN SUFFERING

It is clear by the reference to standing up under suffering that the way out that God provides does not mean an *immediate* end of suffering. The Bible does not promise that God will keep us from all suffering or even remove it quickly; rather, it assures us that He will supply certain provisions, so we can stand strong under the pressure. Trusting in God's faithfulness and promise of a way out is what makes it possible to endure suffering.

Grace and Comfort

God promises to provide the grace and comfort necessary for us to faithfully endure suffering. The psalmist does not say, "Cast your cares on the Lord and go free from care," but rather, "Cast your cares on the LORD and he *will sustain you*" (Ps. 55:22, *NIV*, emphasis added). Similarly, we are not told that the causes of our anxieties will be removed but that in their midst we can experience the peace of God (see Phil. 4:6-7).

During his imprisonment and trial, Paul testified that "the Lord stood with me, and strengthened me" (2 Tim. 4:17). Not only God's strength but also His comfort is available. He is the "Father of mercies and God of all comfort; who comforts us in all our affliction" (2 Cor. 1:3-4).

Joy in Suffering

James wrote, "Consider it all joy, my brethren, when you encounter various trials" (Jas 1:2). But the idea of joy as a result of trials and suffering is not unique to this verse. Paul exhorted, "We also rejoice in our sufferings" (Rom. 5:3, *NIV*). Similarly, Peter said: "Rejoice that you participate in the sufferings of Christ, so that you may be overjoyed when his glory is revealed" (1 Pet. 4:13, *NIV*).

Each of these passages shares part of Jesus' pronouncement, in the Sermon on the Mount, of a state of blessedness (being fortunate, happy or divinely privileged) on the poor, the mourning, the hungry and the persecuted (see Matt. 5:3-4,6,10-12).

These references to joy, or blessedness, in trials and suffering are not for the suffering but for the outcomes. Finding joy in painful trials is possible because we know that "the testing of your faith produces endurance" (Jas. 1:3) and that we are to "let endurance have its perfect result, that you may be perfect [or mature] and complete, lacking in nothing" (Jas. 1:4; see also Rom. 5:3). In the word picture drawn by Peter, trials produce a genuine faith just as a refiner's fire produces gold (see 1 Pet. 1:6-7).

Hope and Assurance

In order to find joy in the midst of trials and suffering, we must have hope. Joy is present because we anticipate future glory. The right attitude in suffering is therefore to focus on hope.

Remember that biblical hope is not wishful thinking but the present assurance of some future good. We do live in a vale of tears, but this is not the end. There is a new day coming for the Christian, a day that is described as fullness of joy where there will be "no more death or mourning or crying or pain, for the old order of things [with its trials and suffering] has passed away" (Rev. 21:4, *NIV*).

The suffering itself helps to build up this view of hope that is so critical for overcoming depression. There is a grand circle in the thinking of Paul in Romans 5 in which hope stands at both ends and tribulation sits in the middle. We "rejoice in the hope of the glory of God" (Rom. 5:2, *NIV*) and we glory in our sufferings because we know that they lead to a sanctifying process that ends in hope. "Suffering produces perseverance; perseverance, character; and character, hope" (Rom. 5:3-4, *NIV*).

Hope not only undergirds our steadfastness in trials and produces joy, but it is also strengthened by such trials. We can accept the sufferings that come our way if we understand their purpose and if we have the hope that God will make things right in the end.

THE PERCEPTION OF GOD'S ABSENCE

What if you could not sense God's presence? What would you do if you were faithfully following God when suddenly your whole life went down the drain? That was the case with Job.

Job was enjoying the benefits of living righteously when one day they were all taken away. His health, wealth and family were all gone! Your mind would spin with questions. *What did I do to deserve this? Did I miss a turn in the road? Is this what I get for living a righteous life? Where is God? God, why are you doing this to me?* Like Job, you would be tempted to curse the day you were born.

It is a marvelous life when we sense the presence of God, live victoriously over sin and know the truth that sets us free. Thank

God for the mountaintop experiences when the circumstances of life are favorable. But are they always?

Something like Job's experience of being stripped of all awareness of God's blessings has happened twice to me (Neil) and my family. Both times preceded significant changes in my ministry. If it was not for the message given in Isaiah 50, I am not sure we would have survived those trials:

> Who is among you that fears the Lord, that obeys the voice of His servant, that walks in darkness and has no light? Let him trust in the name of the Lord and rely on his God. Behold, all you who kindle a fire, who encircle yourselves with firebrands, walk in the light of your fire and among the brands you have set ablaze. This you will have from My hand; and you will lie down in torment (vv. 10-11).

Isaiah is referring to a believer when he asks, "Who is among you that fears the LORD?" He is addressing someone who obeys God and yet walks in darkness. Isaiah is not concerned here about the darkness of sin nor the darkness of this world. He's zeroed in on the darkness of uncertainty, a blanket of heaviness that hovers like a dark cloud over our very being. This darkness comes when the assurance of yesterday has been replaced by the uncertainties of tomorrow and when God has suspended His tangible blessings.

In such a state, even attending church may be a dismal experience. Friends seem more like a bother than a blessing. Could this happen to a true believer? What is the purpose for such a dark time? What is a person to do during these times?

Walk in the Light of Previous Revelation

First, the passage in Job informs us that we are to keep on walking. In the light we can see the next step. We know the difference between a friend and an enemy, and we can see where the obstacles are. The Word is a lamp unto our feet. It provides direction for our steps. In our anguish we may begin to wonder if this is true. Darkness has overcome us. We are embarrassed by how much we rely on feelings rather than light. Every natural instinct tells us to drop out, sit down, stop! But the Scripture encourages us to keep living by faith, according to what we know is true.

The Bible gives us the only infallible rules of faith and knowledge of God, but we learn to live by faith in the arena of life. This is especially true when circumstances are not working in our favor. The Lord has a way of stretching us through a knothole, and just before we are about to break in half, suddenly we slip through to the other side. But we will never go back to the same shape we were in before.

Do Not Create Your Own Light

The second lesson to learn from Isaiah is this: Do not light your own fire. In other words, do not create your own light. The natural tendency, when we do not see things God's way, is to proceed in our way. Notice the text again: "Behold, all you who kindle a fire, who encircle yourselves with firebrands, walk in the light of your fire" (Isa. 50:11). God is not talking about the fire of judgment; He is talking about fire that creates light. Notice what happens when people create their own light: "This you will have from My hand; and you will lie down in torment." Essentially, God is saying, "Go ahead: Do it your way. I'll allow it, but misery will follow."

Let us use an illustration from the Bible. God called Abraham out of Ur into the Promised Land. In Genesis 12, a covenant was made in which God promised Abraham that his descendants would be more numerous than the sands of the sea or the stars in the sky.

Abraham lived his life in the light of that promise and then God turned out the light. So many years passed that his wife, Sarah, could no longer bear a child by natural means. God's guidance had been so clear, but now it looked as though Abraham would have to assist God in its fulfillment.

Who could blame Abraham for creating his own light? Sarah supplied the match by offering her handmaiden to Abraham. Out of that union came another nation that has created so much conflict that the whole world now lies in torment. Jew and Arab have not been able to dwell together peacefully to this day. This all happened because Abraham tried to provide his own light.

God superintended the birth of Moses and provided for his preservation. Raised in the home of Pharaoh, he was given the second most prominent position in Egypt. But God had put into Moses' heart a burden to set his people free. Impulsively, Moses pulled out his sword, attempting to help God. He killed an Egyptian taskmaster, and God turned out the light.

Abandoned to the back side of the desert, Moses spent 40 years tending his father-in-law's sheep. Then one day, he turned and saw a burning bush that was not consumed—God had turned the light back on.

We are not suggesting that we may have to wait 40 years for the cloud to lift. In our life span, that would be more time than an average person's faith could endure. But the darkness may last for weeks, months and, possibly, for some exceptional people, even years. God is in charge, and He knows exactly how small a knothole He can pull each one of us through. We must only remember "the One forming light and creating darkness, causing well-being and creating calamity; I am the LORD who does all these" (Isa. 45:7).

DEPRESSION BUSTERS

Read:

Isaiah 50:10-11

Reflect:

1. How does suffering play a role in our sanctification, our becoming more like Christ?
2. Is suffering inevitable or can it be avoided?
3. Why do you believe some people mistakenly think that Christians should not have to suffer if they live a righteous life?
4. How does hope in the Lord relate to the times we go through suffering when we cannot sense the Lord's presence?

Respond:

Dear Lord, You made it clear that no temptation, testing, trial or suffering can overcome me. God, You are faithful; I know that You will not let me to be tempted or suffer beyond what I can bear. I know that You will always provide a way out for me so that I can stand up under any burden (1 Cor. 10:13, NIV). Lord, thank You for Your great strength and love. At times I don't feel it, but I know it's there, and I know You are there. So I choose to hold on to You and the hope that I have in You, knowing that Your great love will carry me through. In Jesus' name I pray. Amen.

Notes

1. Alice Gray, comp., *Stories for the Extreme Teen's Heart* (Sisters, OR: Multnomah Publishers, 2000), pp. 188-189.
2. Billy Graham, *Unto the Hills* (Nashville, TN: Word Publishing, 1996), n.p.

CHAPTER 12

BACK FROM THE EDGE—A COMMITMENT TO FREEDOM FROM DEPRESSION

For I am convinced that neither death, nor life, nor angels, nor principalities, nor things present, nor things to come, nor powers, nor height, nor depth, nor any other created thing, shall be able to separate us from the love of God, which is in Christ Jesus our Lord.

ROMANS 8:38-39

Forgiveness is the fragrance the violet sheds on the heel that has crushed it.

MARK TWAIN

The apostle John records the story of a man who had been lame for 38 years. The Lord singled him out at the pool of Bethesda, where many other blind, lame and paralyzed people gathered.

The people who were there believed that an angel would occasionally stir the waters and that anybody who was in the pool at the time would be healed. But this poor man could never get to the pool before the waters stopped stirring. "When Jesus saw him lying there and learned that he had been in this condition for a long time, he asked him, 'Do you want to get well?'"(John 5:6, *NIV*).

That is either the cruelest question in the New Testament or one of the most profound. Obviously, it is the latter because Jesus asked it.

The lame man answered:

"I have no one to help me into the pool when the water is stirred. While I am trying to get in, someone else goes down ahead of me." Then Jesus said to him, "Get up! Pick up your mat and walk." At once the man was cured; he picked up his mat and walked (John 5:7-9, *NIV*).

The context suggests that the man probably did not want to get well. He never asked Jesus to be healed, and he had an excuse as to why others could get to the pool and he could not. Later, Jesus found him in the Temple and said to him, "See, you are well again. Stop sinning or something worse may happen to you" (John 5:14, *NIV*). Then the man actually went and told the Jews that it was Jesus who had made him well, turning Him in for healing him on the Sabbath!

When applying this incident to the problem of depression, there are nine commitments to be made if you can answer yes to Jesus' question "Do you want to get well?"

COMMIT YOURSELF TO COMPLETE RECOVERY

> Create in me a clean heart, O God, and renew a steadfast
> spirit within me. Restore to me the joy of Thy salvation,
> and sustain me with a willing spirit (Ps. 51:10,12).

Do you want to get well as much as this psalm indicates King
David did? Are you willing to humble yourself and seek the help
you need from God and others? Are you willing to face the truth
and walk in the light? Do you want a partial answer or the whole
solution?

We ask these tough questions for your sake. More than 50
percent of the people who struggle with depression never ask for
help or seek treatment. There are adequate answers for depression, but you have to want it more than anything and be willing
to do whatever it takes to be free.

The key to any cure is commitment. We are not offering a
Band-Aid, a quick fix or a partial answer. We believe that if you
will follow the procedure in this chapter in the order in which it
comes, you will have a comprehensive and adequate answer for
your depression.

Recovery begins by saying, "I have a problem and I need help."

Recovery begins by saying "I have a problem and I need help." Your diligence in reading to this point demonstrates a commitment to seek the help you need to gain total victory. We have a God of all hope. He is "our refuge and strength, an ever-present help in trouble" (Ps. 46:1, *NIV*). The story of the lame man reveals that God is fully capable of healing someone, even against his will and regardless of his faith. Our heavenly Father will be faithful in all that He has said and in all that He is. "Jesus Christ is the same yesterday and today, yes and forever" (Heb. 13:8).

Commit Yourself to Prayer

Do not be anxious about anything, but in everything, by prayer and petition, with thanksgiving, present your requests to God. And the peace of God, which transcends all understanding, will guard your hearts and your minds in Christ Jesus (Phil. 4:6-7, *NIV*).

We are asking you to *pray*, not to get tough and try harder. That kind of advice and attitude could itself lead to burnout and depression.

Human effort alone will not be an adequate answer. Besides, adding one more thing to your plate would only contribute to your crisis, not solve it. Instead, we are encouraging you to trust God by submitting yourself to Him and His ways and by seeking a holistic answer through the godly counsel and assistance of others.

If you have the desire to get well and if you are willing to assume your responsibility for your own attitudes and actions, then we believe there is hope for you.

He alone can bind up the brokenhearted and set the captive free. God can do wonders with a broken heart if you give Him all the pieces. The world will encourage you to seek every possible natural explanation and cure before you consider God. When that is not successful, people will say "There is nothing more that we can do but pray." Scripture has a different order. "But seek first His kingdom and His righteousness; and all these things shall be added to you" (Matt. 6:33).

The first thing a Christian should do about anything is pray. May we suggest that you read aloud the prayer at the end of this chapter in the response section to begin your process of recovery?

COMMIT TO AN INTIMATE RELATIONSHIP WITH GOD

Come to me, all you who are weary and burdened, and I will give you rest. Take my yoke upon you and learn from me, for I am gentle and humble in heart, and you will find rest for your souls. For my yoke is easy and my burden is light (Matt. 11:28-30, *NIV*).

A whole answer will require the presence of God in your life. Jesus is not just a "higher power"; He is our Lord and Savior who took upon Himself the form of a man and dwelt among us. He was tempted in every way and suffered a humiliating and agonizing death so that we could have access to our heavenly Father.

Jesus says, "Come. Come to Me." We are being invited into the very presence of God. We need His presence in our lives because He is our life. We must do what is recorded in Hebrews 10:22-25 (*NIV*):

Let us draw near to God with a sincere heart in full assurance of faith, having our hearts sprinkled to cleanse us from a guilty conscience and having our bodies washed with pure water. Let us hold unswervingly to the hope we profess, for he who promised is faithful. And let us consider how we may spur one another on toward love and good deeds. Let us not give up meeting together, as some are in the habit of doing, but let us encourage one another—and all the more as you see the Day approaching.

The greatest crisis humankind has ever suffered was when Adam and Eve lost their relationship with God. The ultimate answer is to reestablish an intimate relationship with Him who is our only hope. What Adam and Eve lost was life. Jesus came to give it back.

We possess that spiritual and eternal life the moment we are born again. That relationship was established by the blood of Christ and His resurrection. We need to maintain that relationship by living in harmony with our heavenly Father. This may require resolving certain personal and spiritual conflicts between ourselves and God.

The Steps to Freedom in Christ (found in Neil's book *Finding Hope Again*) is intended to help you resolve these conflicts through repentance and faith in Him.

Essentially, the process assists you in submitting to God and resisting the devil (see Jas. 4:7). This removes the influence of the enemy in your life and connects you with God in a personal and powerful way. You will then be able to experience the peace of God that guards your heart and mind (see Phil. 4:7), and you will sense the Holy Spirit's bearing witness with your spirit (see Rom. 8:16). With this understanding and by the grace of God, you will be able to grasp the remaining issues in this chapter.

Many people will be able to walk through these Steps to Freedom without outside help, because Jesus is the Wonderful

Counselor. The likelihood of your gaining freedom will be greatly increased, however, if you first read Neil and Dave's books *Stomping Out the Darkness* and *The Bondage Breaker,* Youth Edition.

Before you go through the Steps to Freedom, find a quiet place where you will not be interrupted and you can be alone with God. Give yourself three to four hours. You have nothing to lose by going through this process of submitting to God and resisting the devil, and you have a lot to gain.

The Steps to Freedom in Christ are nothing more than a fierce moral inventory intended to help you clean house and make room for Jesus to reign in His temple. There is one major caution, however. In our experience, severe cases will require the assistance of a godly encourager. If you really want to get well, you will not hesitate to ask a Christ-centered pastor or counselor for help.

COMMIT YOURSELF

How great is the love the Father has lavished on us, that we should be called children of God! And that is what we are! The reason the world does not know us is that it did not know him. Dear friends, now we are children of God, and what we will be has not yet been made known. But we know that when he appears, we shall be like him, for we shall see him as he is. Everyone who has this hope in him purifies himself, just as he is pure (1 John 3:1-3, *NIV*).

Knowing who God is and who we are in Christ are the two most essential beliefs that enable us to live a victorious life. God loves you because He is love. It is His nature to love you. He could not do anything else.

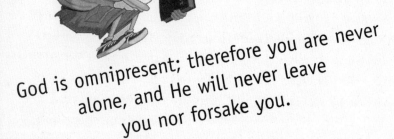

God is omnipresent; therefore you are never alone, and He will never leave you nor forsake you.

As we wrote in chapter 5, God is omnipotent. Therefore you can do all things through Christ who strengthens you (see Phil. 4:13). God is omniscient. Therefore, He knows the thoughts and intentions of your heart (see Heb. 4:12-13). He knows your needs and is able to meet every one.

God is omnipresent. Therefore, you are never alone, and He will never leave you nor forsake you. You have become a partaker of His divine nature (see 2 Pet. 1:4), because your soul is in union with Him. That is what it means to be spiritually alive *in* Christ. He has defeated the devil, forgiven your sins and given you eternal life. You are now His child if you have received Him into your life. "To all who received him, to those who believed in his name, he gave the right to become children of God" (John 1:12, *NIV*). If the devil wanted to discourage you, all he would have to do is get you to believe a lie about who God is and who you are in Christ.

Recall King David's depression, as expressed in Psalm 13:1-2: "How long, O LORD? Wilt Thou forget me forever? How long wilt Thou hide thy face from me? How long shall I take counsel in my soul, having sorrow in my heart all the day? How long will my enemy be exalted over me?"

David is depressed because what he believes about God is not true, and there goes his hope. An omniscient God could not forget him even for a moment, much less forever! And who is David taking counsel with? Himself! There are no answers there.

The *New International Version* translates "take counsel with my soul" as "wrestle with my thoughts." All depressed young people wrestle with their thoughts. Negative self-talk only fuels Satan's forces in the battle for the mind. We must take every thought captive to the obedience of Christ (see 2 Cor. 10:5) and then choose to think upon that which is true (see Phil. 4:8).

Notice how David overcomes his depression: "But I trust in your unfailing love; my heart rejoices in your salvation. I will sing to the LORD, for he has been good to me" (Ps. 13:5-6, *NIV*). David overcomes his depression by turning to God, who loves him, and by recalling to his mind the good that God has done for him.

Then David chooses to sing to the Lord. The immediate result of being filled with the Spirit is to give thanks, sing and make melody in our hearts to the Lord (see Eph. 5:18-20). That is an act of the will we can all freely exercise. Singing Christian hymns and choruses helps us refocus our minds.

We strongly suggest that you flood your mind with Christian songs and choruses and stop listening to dark and destructive music.

The appendix of this book includes a list of Scripture verses that affirm who you are in Christ and show how He meets our need for acceptance, security and significance. The appendix also includes an Overcomer's Covenant, based on your position in Christ. When you feel discouraged and depressed, these will help you refocus your mind on the truth of who you are in Christ and the position you have in Him.

Recall that this is what Jeremiah did in Lamentations 3:21-24 (*NIV*):

Yet this I call to mind and therefore I have hope: Because of the LORD's great love we are not consumed, for his compassions never fail. They are new every morning; great is your faithfulness. I say to myself, "The LORD is my portion; therefore I will wait for Him."

COMMIT YOUR BODY TO GOD

Therefore, I urge you, brothers, in view of God's mercy, to offer your bodies as living sacrifices, holy and pleasing to God—this is your spiritual act of worship (Rom. 12:1, *NIV*).

Do you not know that your body is a temple of the Holy Spirit, who is in you, whom you have received from God? You are not your own; you were bought at a price. Therefore honor God with your body (1 Cor. 6:19-20, *NIV*).

Depression is a multifaceted problem that affects the body, soul and spirit. Consequently, a comprehensive cure for depression will require a whole answer. There are many forms of *biological* depression, and most can be detected by a comprehensive medical exam. However, a 10-minute checkup will not be sufficient nor will a visit to a psychiatrist who only reads the symptoms to prescribe antidepressant medication. There is no precise way to measure brain chemistry.

If your depression is truly endogenous (originating within your body), you need some evidence to validate any medical treatment. Find a medical doctor or psychiatrist who can administer the appropriate tests and who understands the value of good nutrition.

Medical tests for most conditions related to depression are fairly routine and effective. In addition, each of us should assume personal responsibility for finding the proper balance of rest, exercise and diet. To live a healthy life, we must be health oriented, not illness oriented.

We see the same dynamic in winning the battle for the mind. The answer is not to renounce all the lies. The answer is to choose the truth. But if we are not aware that lies exist and if we ignore what our bodies tell us, then we will likely fall victim to the father of lies and the disease.

If you sense that you are physically and mentally slipping back into a depression, do not just give in to it; take charge of your life by praying as follows:

Dear heavenly Father, I submit myself to You as Your child, and I declare myself to be totally dependent upon You. I yield my body to You as a living sacrifice, and I ask You to fill me with Your Holy Spirit. I renounce the lies of the evil one and I choose to believe the truth as You have revealed it to us in Your holy Word. Give me the grace and the wisdom to resist the devil so that he will flee from me. I now commit myself to You, including my body as an instrument of righteousness. In Jesus' precious name I pray. Amen.

COMMIT YOURSELF TO THE RENEWING OF YOUR MIND

Do not conform any longer to the pattern of this world, but be transformed by the renewing of your mind. Then you will be able to test and approve what God's will is— his good, pleasing and perfect will (Rom. 12:2, *NIV*).

Depression can be related to lifestyle or brought on by some crisis event. By lifestyle depression we mean a depressive state that began in early childhood or has existed for many years. It is possible that lifestyle depression can have hereditary connections. That possibility is more likely with bipolar than unipolar depression. In such cases, medication may be required for complete recovery, but always seek out godly counsel as well.

It is far more common, however, for the cause of lifestyle depression to be traceable to early childhood development or living in an oppressive situation that created or communicated a sense of hopelessness and helplessness.

Learned helplessness can be unlearned by the renewing of our minds. Over time, our computerlike brains have been programmed to think negatively about ourselves, our circumstances and the future. These negative thoughts and lies have been deeply ingrained. Thousands and thousands of prior mental rehearsals have added to the feelings we have right now.

How can we win the battle for our minds? Should we rebuke every negative thought? No! If we tried, that is all we would be doing for the rest of our lives. We would be like a person stuck in the middle of a lake with 12 corks floating around our head and a little hammer in our hand. All our energy would be expended trying to keep the corks submerged with the hammer, while trying to tread water. We should ignore the corks and swim to shore.

Similarly, we overcome the father of lies by choosing the truth. You can do that if you have successfully submitted to God and resisted the devil. If you have not, then you are bopping corks and treading water.

There is a major difference between *winning* the spiritual battle for your mind and the long-term growth process of *renewing* your mind. It does not take long to establish your freedom in Christ, but it will take the rest of your life to renew your mind

It does not take long to establish your freedom in Christ, but it will take the rest of your life to renew your mind and conform to the image of God.

and conform to the image of God. Although getting free in Christ can happen in a relatively short period of time, there is no such thing as instant maturity.

Changing false beliefs and attitudes is necessary to overcome depression. The world will put you down, and the devil will accuse you, but you do not have to believe either one. You must take every thought captive to the obedience of Christ. In other words, you have to believe the truth as revealed in God's Word. You do not overcome the father of lies by research or by reason but by revelation. To this end, Jesus petitioned our heavenly Father in His high priestly prayer on our behalf:

> I am coming to you [God] now, but I say these things while I am still in the world, so that they may have the full measure of my joy within them. I have given them your word and the world has hated them, for they are not of the world any more than I am of the world. My prayer is not that you take them out of the world but that you protect them from the evil one. They are not of

the world, even as I am not of it. Sanctify them by the truth; your word is truth (John 17:13-17, *NIV*).

God is not going to remove us from the negativity of this fallen world, but we are sanctified and protected by the truth of His Word. Jesus said, "These things I have spoken to you, that in Me you may have peace. In the world you have tribulation, but take courage; I have overcome the world" (John 16:33).

Renewing our minds with truth is fairly easy, but this renewal will not continue if we do not actively work to sustain it. David said in Psalm 119:15-16, "I will meditate on Thy precepts, and regard Thy ways. I shall delight in Thy statutes; I shall not forget Thy word."

Every mental stronghold that is torn down in Christ makes the next one easier to dismantle. Every thought we take captive makes the next one more likely to surrender. Lifestyle depression is the result of repeated blows that come from living in a fallen world. Rehearsing the truth again and again is the key to renewing our minds.

COMMIT YOURSELF TO GOOD BEHAVIOR

The things you have learned and received and heard and seen in me, practice these things; and the God of peace shall be with you (Phil. 4:9).

No one can be instantly delivered from lifestyle depression; everyone who suffers from it must grow out of it.

And the LORD had regard for Abel and his offering; but for Cain and for his offering He had no regard. So Cain became very angry and his countenance fell. Then the LORD said to Cain, "Why are you angry? And why has your countenance fallen? If you do well, will not your countenance be lifted up? And if you do not do well, sin is crouching at the door; and its desire is for you, but you must master it" (Gen. 4:4-7).

In other words, we do not *feel* our way into good behavior, we *behave* our way into a good feeling. If we wait until we feel like doing what is right, we will likely never do it. Jesus said, "If you know these things, you are blessed *if you do them*" (John 13:17, emphasis added).

That is why much of the initial intervention for severe depression focuses on behavior. Schedule appointments and activities that pull you out of your negative mood. Force yourself to work, even though you may not feel like getting out of bed. Plan an activity and stick to it. Commit yourself to getting more exercise, and follow through. Start with a low-impact aerobic program or take walks with friends and family members. Continue routine duties even though you feel as if you do not have the energy.

These behavioral interventions or activities are only a start in developing a lifestyle that is healthy. If these are too difficult or physically impossible, then seek the kind of medical help that will get you back on your feet.

Watch for certain negative behaviors that will only contribute to depression. Drowning out your sorrows with drugs and alcohol is at the top of this destructive list.

COMMIT YOURSELF TO MEANINGFUL RELATIONSHIPS

And let us consider how to stimulate one another to love and good deeds, not forsaking our own assembling together, as is the habit of some, but encouraging one another; and all the more, as you see the day drawing near (Heb. 10:24-25).

One of the major symptoms of depression is withdrawal from meaningful relationships. Isolating yourself so you are alone with your negative thoughts will certainly contribute to a downward spiral.

You may feel that you need to be alone; however, you need to stay in contact with the responsible people. Wrong associations will only pull you down. "Do not be deceived: 'Bad company corrupts good morals'" (1 Cor. 15:33). We suggest that you go see your youth pastor or find another godly youth pastor in your community. Tell him or her the struggle you are having with depression and ask what the church offers in terms of youth fellowship. A good church will have many meaningful activities and small discipleship groups where you can get the prayer and care you need.

Anybody who has suffered from lifestyle depression for any length of time will have people in their lives that they need to forgive, and some that need reconciliation. We hope you resolve the need to forgive others as you go through the Steps to Freedom. Concerning the need to seek the forgiveness of others, Jesus said, "If therefore you are presenting your offering at the altar, and there remember that your brother has something against you, leave your offering there before the altar, and go your way; first be reconciled to your brother, and then come and present your offering" (Matt. 5:23-24).

If you need to be forgiven of your sins, then go to God. But if you have offended or hurt someone else, do not go to God first. Go to that person and be reconciled. You will have little mental peace until you do both.

COMMIT YOURSELF TO OVERCOME EVERY LOSS

But whatever things were gain to me, those things I have counted as loss for the sake of Christ. More than that, I count all things to be loss in view of the surpassing value of knowing Christ Jesus my Lord, for whom I have suffered the loss all things, and count them but rubbish in order that I may gain Christ (Phil. 3:7-8).

DEPRESSION BUSTERS

Read:

Romans 8:31-39

Reflect:

1. In John 5:7-9 the man by the well really didn't want to get well. Why is it so important that you have a true desire to get well before you can overcome depression?
2. Why does recovery over depression begin by saying, "I have a problem and I need help?" What happens if you don't?
3. Why are prayer and commitment to an intimate relationship with Jesus so important to your recovery?
4. Read through the "Who I Am in Christ" list and "The Overcomer's Covenant in Christ" (in the appendix);

then select a key verse or verses and one key phrase that stands out to you and memorize them.

Respond:

Dear heavenly Father, I come to You as Your child. I declare my total dependence upon You and acknowledge that apart from Christ I can do nothing. Thank You for sending Jesus to die in my place in order that my sins could be forgiven. I praise You for Your resurrection power that raised Jesus from the grave in order that I too might have eternal life.

I choose to believe the truth that the devil has been defeated and that I am now seated with Christ in the heavenlies. Therefore, I choose to believe that I have the power and the authority to do Your will and be the person You created me to be. I submit my body to You as a living sacrifice and ask You to fill me with Your Holy Spirit. I desire nothing more than to know and do your will, believing that it is good, perfect and acceptable for me. I invite the Spirit of truth to lead me into all truth that I may be set free in Christ. I choose from this day forward to walk in the light and speak the truth in love. I acknowledge my pain to You and confess my sins, doubts and lack of trust. I now invite You to search my heart, try my ways and see if there is any wicked way within me; then lead me into the everlasting way by the power and guidance of Your Holy Spirit. In Jesus' precious name I pray. Amen.

WHO I AM IN CHRIST

I AM ACCEPTED

John 1:12	I am God's child.
John 15:15	I am Christ's friend.
Romans 5:1	I have been justified.
1 Corinthians 6:17	I am united with the Lord, and I am one spirit with Him.
1 Corinthians 6:20	I have been bought with a price. I belong to God.
1 Corinthians 12:27	I am a member of Christ's Body.
Ephesians 1:1	I am a saint.
Ephesians 1:5	I have been adopted as God's child.
Ephesians 2:18	I have direct access to God through the Holy Spirit.
Colossians 1:14	I have been redeemed and forgiven of all my sins.
Colossians 2:10	I am complete in Christ.

I AM SECURE

Romans 8:1-2	I am free from condemnation.
Romans 8:28	I am assured that all things work together for good.
Romans 8:31-34	I am free from any condemning charges against me.
Romans 8:35-39	I cannot be separated from the love of God.
2 Corinthians 1:21-22	I have been established, anointed and sealed by God.
Colossians 3:3	I am hidden with Christ in God.
Philippians 1:6	I am confident that the good work God has begun in me will be perfected.
Philippians 3:20	I am a citizen of heaven.
2 Timothy 1:7	I have not been given a spirit of fear, but of power, love and a sound mind.
Hebrews 4:16	I can find grace and mercy to help in time of need.
1 John 5:18	I am born of God and the evil one cannot touch me.

I AM SIGNIFICANT

Matthew 5:13-14	I am the salt and light of the earth.
John 15:1,5	I am a branch of the true vine, a channel of His life.
John 15:16	I have been chosen and appointed to bear fruit.
Acts 1:8	I am a personal witness of Christ.
1 Corinthians 3:16	I am God's temple.
2 Corinthians 5:17-21	I am a minister of reconciliation for God.
2 Corinthians 6:1	I am God's coworker (see 1 Corinthians 3:9).
Ephesians 2:6	I am seated with Christ in the heavenly realm.
Ephesians 2:10	I am God's workmanship.
Ephesians 3:12	I may approach God with freedom and confidence.
Philippians 4:13	I can do all things through Christ who strengthens me.

THE OVERCOMER'S COVENANT IN CHRIST

1. I place all my trust and confidence in the Lord, I put no confidence in the flesh and I declare myself to be dependent upon God.

2. I consciously and deliberately choose to submit to God and resist the devil by denying myself, picking up my cross daily and following Jesus.

3. I choose to humble myself before the mighty hand of God in order that He may exalt me at the proper time.

4. I declare the truth that I am dead to sin, freed from it and alive to God in Christ Jesus, since I have died with Christ and was raised with Him.

5. I gladly embrace the truth that I am now a child of God who is unconditionally loved and accepted. I reject the lie that I have to perform to be accepted, and I reject my fallen and natural identity which was derived from the world.

6. I declare that sin shall no longer be master over me because I am not under the law, but under grace, and there is no more guilt or condemnation because I am spiritually alive in Christ Jesus.

7. I renounce every unrighteous use of my body and I commit myself to no longer be conformed to this world, but rather to be transformed by the renewing of my mind. I choose to believe the truth and walk in it, regardless of my feelings or circumstances.

8. I commit myself to take every thought captive to the obedience of Christ, and choose to think upon that which is true, honorable, right, pure and lovely.

9. I commit myself to God's great goal for my life to conform to His image. I know that I will face many trials, but God has given me the victory and I am not a victim, but an overcomer in Christ.

10. I choose to adopt the attitude of Christ, which was to do nothing from selfishness or empty conceit, but with humility of mind. I will regard others as more important than myself; and not merely look out for my own personal interests but also the interests of others. I know that it is more blessed to give than to receive.

Help Is on the Way

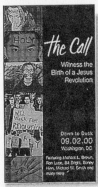
 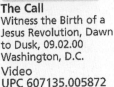

Keep the Faith

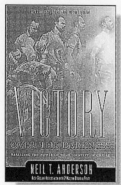

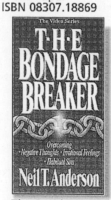
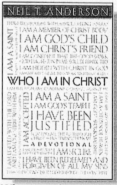

Freedom in Christ Resources

Part One: *Resolving Personal Conflicts**

Victory over the Darkness
Start here! This best-seller combined with *The Bondage Breaker* will show you how to find your freedom in Christ. Realize the power of your identity in Christ!
Paperback • 239 pp. B001
Study Guide • Paper • 153 pp. G001

Daily in Christ
by Neil and Joanne Anderson
This uplifting 365-day devotional will encourage, motivate and challenge you to live *Daily in Christ*. There's a one-page devotional and brief heartfelt prayer for each day. Celebrate and experience your freedom all year.
Paperback • 365 pp. B010

Breaking Through to Spiritual Maturity
This is a dynamic Group Study of *Victory over the Darkness* and *The Bondage Breaker*. Complete with teaching notes for a 13-week (or 26-week) Bible study, with reproducible handouts. Ideal for Sunday School classes, Bible studies and discipleship groups.
Paperback • 151 pp. G003

Victory over the Darkness Video & Audio
In this, the first half of his "basic training" seminar, Neil Anderson explores how to resolve personal conflicts through discovering one's identity in Christ, embracing the ministry of reconciliation, experiencing emotional freedom and more.
Videotape Set • 8 lessons V031
Audiotape Set • 8 lessons A031
Audio-CD Set • 8 lessons CD031
Audiobook • 180 min. A035
Workbook • Paper 20pp. W009

Overcoming Negative Self Image
Focuses on self-esteem issues and reveals the truth about what God thinks of us and who we are because of Christ. You + Christ = wholeness and meaning.
Paperback • 112 pp. B001-1

Overcoming Addictive Behavior
Teaches the unique, Christ-centered model for recovery that has already helped hundreds of thousands break free from various addictive behaviors.
Paperback • 160 pp. B001-2

Who I Am in Christ
36 readings and prayers based on scriptural passages that assure us of God's love and our security and freedom in His kingdom.
Paperback • 288 pp. B03

Part Two: *Resolving Spiritual Conflicts**

The Bondage Breaker
This best-seller combines the definitive process of breaking bondages with the *Steps to Freedom in Christ*. Read this with *Victory over the Darkness* and you will be able to resolve your personal and spiritual conflicts.
Paperback • 302 pp. B002
Study Guide • Paper • 139 pp. G002

The Steps to Freedom in Christ
This is a handy version of *The Steps to Freedom in Christ*, the discipleship counseling process from *The Bondage Breaker*. It is ideal for personal use or for helping another person who wants to find his or her freedom.
Booklet • 36 pp. G004

The Steps to Freedom in Christ Video
In this special video experience, Dr. Neil Anderson personally leads you or a loved one through the bondage-breaking Steps to Freedom in Christ in the privacy of your living room. Includes *The Steps to Freedom in Christ* booklet.
Videotape • 70 minutes V010

Praying by the Power of the Holy Spirit
"If prayer is so important, why is it so difficult?" Neil Anderson explores how we can intimately connect with our loving heavenly Father. End of chapter questions help with application and are ideal for group study.
Paperback • 100pp. B002-1

Finding God's Will in Spiritually Deceptive Times
Does God's message come through other people, throughout Scripture, or both? The answer must be based on two powerful truths: We are alive in Christ, and we are God's children. Includes questions for group study or discussion
Paperback • 100pp. B002-2

All titles by Neil Anderson unless otherwise indicated.

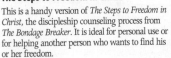

Freedom in Christ Resources

Part Two Continued*

Spiritual Warfare
by Dr. Timothy Warner

This concise book offers balanced, biblical insights on spiritual warfare, with practical information and ammunition for winning the spiritual battle. Every reader will benefit by learning from the author's extensive experience.

Paperback • 160 pp. B007

The Bondage Breaker Video & Audio

In this, the second half of his "basic training" seminar, Neil Anderson explores how to resolve spiritual conflicts through the authority and protection God provides, living free in Christ, training believers to resist temptation and more.

Videotape Set • 360 minutes V032
Audiotape Set • 8 lessons A032
Audio-CD Set • 8 lessons CD032
Audiobook • 180 min. A057
Workbook • Paper 20pp. W010

Part Three: *Discipleship Counseling*

Discipleship Counseling

A guide for church leaders and those involved in counseling to understand how discipleship counseling works and how to create such a ministry in their own church.

Paperback • 425 pp. B036

Helping Others Find Freedom in Christ Video Training Program

This Video Training Program is a complete training kit for churches and groups who want to establish a freedom ministry using *The Steps to Freedom in Christ*. Includes four 45-minute video lessons.

Video Training Program • V015

Freedom in Christ Discipleship Counseling

This series presents advanced counseling insights and practical, biblical answers to help others find their freedom in Christ. It is the full content from Dr. Anderson's advanced seminar of the same name.

Videotape Set • 8 lessons V033
Audiotape Set • 8 lessons A033
Audio-CD Set • 8 lessons CD033
Workbook • Paper 24pp. W011

Setting Your Church Free
by Neil Anderson and Charles Mylander

This powerful book reveals how pastors and church leaders can lead their entire churches to freedom by discovering the key issues of both corporate bondage and corporate freedom. A must-read for every church leader.

Paperback • 352 pp. B013

Topical Resources*

Freedom from Addiction
by Neil Anderson and Mike and Julia Quarles

A book like no other on true recovery! This unique Christ-centered model has helped thousands break free alcoholism, drug addiction and other addictive behaviors. The Quarles's amazing story will encourage every reader!

Paperback • 356 pp. B019
Workbook • Paper • 206pp G019

Freedom from Addiction Video Study
by Neil Anderson and Mike and Julia Quarles

A dynamic resource for recovery group leading pastors and Christian counselors. A step-by-step study that changes lives. Includes video study, paperback and workbook.

Video Study • V019

Finding Hope Again
by Neil Anderson & Hal Baumchen

With the number of people seeking medical treatment for depression doubling in the last decade, we are clearly experiencing an epidemic that medication alone will not cure. *Finding Hope Again* offers a biblically-based and Christ-centered answer that addresses the whole person.

Paperback 330pp. B026
Video Set 8 lessons V034
Audio Set 8 lessons A034
Audio-CD Set • 8 lessons CD034
Workbook • Paper • 25 pp. W012

Breaking the Bondage of Legalism

According to a recent poll, 57 percent of Christians strongly agree the Christian life is well summed up as "trying hard what God commands," but biblically, making laws our "lord" estranges us from Christ.   Find the keys to liberty: our identity in Christ.

Paperback • 300 pp. B009

God's Power at Work in You
by Neil Anderson and Robert Saucy

Anderson and Saucy deal with the dangerous common misconceptions that hinder spiritual growth, including: How can we overcome sin and resist temptation? What is God's role in helping us stay pure? What is our role? What is the key to consistent victory?

Paperback • B032

Released from Bondage

This book shares true stories of freedom from obsessive thoughts, compulsive behaviors, guilt, satanic ritual abuse, childhood abuse and demonic strongholds, combined with helpful commentary from Dr. Anderson.

Paperback • 258 pp. B006

All titles by Neil Anderson unless otherwise indicated.

Freedom in Christ Resources

Topical Resources Continued*

Rivers of Revival
by Neil Anderson and Elmer L. Towns

Answers what many Christians are asking today: "What will it take to see revival?" Examines the fascinating subject of personal revival and past and current evangelistic streams that could help usher in global revival.

Hardcover • 288 pp. B023

A Way of Escape

Talking about sex is never easy. This vital book provides real answers for sexual struggles, unwanted thoughts, compulsive habits or a painful past. Don't learn to just cope; learn how to resolve your sexual issues in Christ.

Paperback • 238 pp. B014

The Christ-Centered Marriage
by Neil Anderson and Charles Mylander

Husbands and wives, discover and enjoy your freedom in Christ together! Break free from old habit patterns and enjoy greater intimacy, joy and fulfillment.

Paperback • 300 pp. B025
Study Guide • Paper • 200 pp. SG020

Parenting Resources*

Spiritual Protection for Your Children
by Neil Anderson and Peter and Sue VanderHook

The fascinating true story of an average middle-class American family's spiritual battle on the home front, and the lessons we can all learn about protecting our families from the enemy's attacks. Includes helpful prayers for children of various ages.

Paperback • 300 pp. B021

The Seduction of Our Children

This parenting book and series will change the way you view the spiritual development of your children. Helpful insights are offered on many parenting issues such as discipline, communication and spiritual oversight of children. A panel of experts share their advice.

Paperback • 245 pp. B004
Additional workbooks • 49 pp. W004

Youth Resources*

Stomping Out the Darkness
by Neil Anderson and Dave Park

This youth version of *Victory over the Darkness* shows youth how to break free and discover the joy of their identity in Christ. (Part 1 of 2.)

Paperback • 210 pp. B101
Study Guide • Paper • 137 pp. G101

The Bondage Breaker Youth Edition
by Neil Anderson and Dave Park

This youth best-seller shares the process of breaking bondages and the *Youth Steps to Freedom in Christ*. Read this with *Stomping Out the Darkness*. (Part 2 of 2.)

Paperback • 248 pp. B102
Study Guide • Paper • 128 pp. G102

Busting Free!
by Neil Anderson and Dave Park

This is a dynamic group study of *Stomping Out the Darkness* and *The Bondage Breaker Youth Edition*. It has complete teaching notes for a 13-week (or 26-week) Bible study, with reproducible handouts. Ideal for Sunday School classes, Bible studies and youth discipleship groups of all kinds.

Manual • 163 pp. G103

Leading Teens to Freedom in Christ
by Neil Anderson and Rich Miller

This youth version provides comprehensive, hands-on biblical discipleship counseling training for parents, youth workers and youth pastors, equipping them to help young people.

Paperback • 300 pp. B112

Purity Under Pressure
by Neil Anderson and Dave Park

Real answers for real world pressures! Youth will find out the difference between being friends, dating and having a relationship. No hype, no big lectures; just straightforward talk about living free in Christ.

Paperback • 200 pp. B104

Youth Devotionals
by Neil Anderson along with Rich Miller, Dave Park or Robert Saucy.

These four 40-day devotionals help young people understand God's love and their identity in Christ. Teens will learn to establish a positive spiritual habit of getting into God's Word on a daily basis.

Extreme Faith
Paperback
200 pp. B108

Awesome God
Paperback
200 pp. B108

Reality Check
Paperback
200 pp. B107

Ultimate Love
Paperback
209 pp. B109

Real Life
Paperback
200 pp. B115

Sold Out for God
Paperback
200 pp. B116

Righteous Pursuit
Paperback
200 pp. B114

*All titles by Neil Anderson unless otherwise indicated.